# The 1
# I Saw You

## Poetry For Lovers

# W. Blaine Wheeler

**outskirts press**

For my lover and wife, Nadia.

# Contents

I
Prologues
Page 1

II
Melodies
Page 43

III
Symphonies
Page 91

IV
Longings
Page 133

V
Odes to Hope
Page 189

VI
Epilogues
Page 217

# I
## Prologues

# 1

Windy heights on Sunday castles
    with afternoons
    too rare
    force yesterdays
    from our separated hands
And bring thoughts of tomorrows reaching
Beyond all todays
    with voices of I may fall
    gently echoed by
    I will hold you.

# 2

The magical moment I met you will live
    forever
    in my mind
As you appeared from the mists
    of despair
    bringing hope
To me who had given up all thoughts
    of hope
    in my life.
Loving much more than your lovely self
    touched
    my being.
Stay and remove
The burdens of my past
With your joyful
Words sounding in my heart.

How could I know if you
    were waiting
    for me
When you never told me
    that you
    were waiting
    for me.
Never doubting that I would
    always
    be waiting
For the only love of my life?

Now comes the time when
Aloneness
Deadens our hearts to
Intimacies dreams cannot
Allay.

Spray-blowing fountains entertained and
    stiff-gaited pigeons walked near a bench
Warmed by an afternoon London sun
Where two ate, talked, and laughed
    as the beginnings of a September
    day of discovery
    unfolded so easily.
Manners of the British and serpentine Moores

Contributed more than they can know
    to two who wanted
    more than they had
    that day
When letters and calls of the past became real.
And on into the evening
    touching,
    hoping,
    and finding
Memories shared of another year
Not strange
But familiar through desires born
    beyond need
    rising and bursting
    covering both
With peace and strength and dreams.


6


I waited my whole
    life
    for you
Knowing love is meant to be shared
As it invites wonder
And leads each on new paths
    to explore
While lifting the other up when fallen;
All the while understanding that
    the wait
    for you
Was much more than mere time.

7

We never wanted our first day together
    to end
When there seemed not enough time
    to find
What we each had been searching for
During those years of not knowing
What we each had so fully not
    found.
We now wonder in good amazement
What gods or forces or urges kept
Us from touching each other that day,
    our first day,
When abundantly our hearts were
    joined
By something larger than we were
    our first day
    of wonderous discovery.

8

When you had to create an absence
    that evening
    far too soon
After we first met without our knowing
    beyond
Our racing joys of having with unspoken thoughts
Known that we each belonged to the other,
Did you hold in your
    sad heart
What I held so fearlessly
    in mine?

9

Our early embers became soon
    for each
Consuming flames replenished by
    our need
Of burning dances then and on through
    our night
Knowing that love speaks in ways
The other can fully understand.

We relinquished our dreams easily
    without hesitation
Because then the reality of our hands
    on each
Gave birth to a good realization that
    those dreams
Had given way to a presence made
So firmly and freely from each.


10

So early you deserved to know
    where
I would find you.
There was no emptiness of thought
In my innocence as I joyfully
Looked into my captured heart
    enchanted
Not by a soft vision
But by a hope I had never had.

I found you everywhere I searched
And I was never lost.

## 11

You knew before I was able to see
      as you told me
That very first time of our ever meeting
Oh, it is you.

How did you know and perhaps also
Why did you recognize me as the
      one of your life
That afternoon when all I could do
Was stand speechlessly in mute
      adoration?

## 12

I knew I was not mistaken that afternoon
      there among stately trees
      on the grounds
      of the old cathedral
Where we found ourselves laughing so well
After the careful trip from your lovely home
      on the bus
      where we
      never touched.

I saw you sitting on a bench seemingly
In thought of other vistas and other hopes
While I wondered how I could intrude
      without disturbing
      your moments
Which I wanted to be fully a part of
Never realizing that all along we were

To be part of the emotions we had hidden
    from the other.

We held each other closely that afternoon
    without a word
    without a touch
Knowing that what stirred deeply in each
Was not a mistake but the beginning
    of a love
    we had never had.


## 13

I know you remember saying that day
    of almost harm
That you cannot give up on me;
And I can never forget what I said
    to my only love:
That I will fight for you the only one
    of my life.
Our care for each that day when solemn
    assurances
Were not only given but truly accepted
Became the fertile ground for all we
    are now.


## 14

Did my search ever begin for you
    my only one,
Or were we perhaps always together

Without realizing that knowing of the other
    just was?
What we do know without needing to say
Is that our union has filled each
    with delight
And that there is no need to ask when
Did we not know this binding of our hearts.

## 15

How we have waited for our day,
    and now no more goodbyes;
Knowing we would finally be together,
    and now no more goodbyes;
Seeing only joyous visions of our future,
    and now no more goodbyes;
Finding life is always each other,
    and now no more goodbyes;
Finally seeing you in your wedding dress,
    and now no more goodbyes;
Telling each there will be a forever,
    and now no more goodbyes;
    and now no more goodbyes.

## 16

When I had no hope, you held me
    closely
So that I would know the happiness of
    love.
What you gave me in those days of our
    beginnings

Was far more than all hope my dreams could
    find.


## 17

I will always wake up to you
    knowing in my heart
    that you want me
    next to you
As we walk and laugh together
Through another day of love and joy
Keeping each other in our hearts.


## 18

The nearness of you our first day
    removed both
    my breath
    and my voice
Because you caused so easily my heart
To beat faster than it ever had
    for any reason.


## 19

    Holding only you:
    Kissing only you;
    Loving only you;
    These are now
    My truest life.

## 20

When you told me that sad day that
 you had to leave,
I was saddened beyond all my experience
For I had never known this before.

You took my entire heart with you
 as you left me
Telling me that all you could leave me
Was your warm heart to keep.

More than an apart and hard year later,
 you returned to me
Bearing my heart which you kept
As we then forever united our hearts.

## 21

You must know that I will be
 needing you
 always and forever
As each morning I awaken finding you
 next to me
Knowing you will always be mine.

## 22

This yearning I feel holds me as nothing
 before,
And I am unable to remove from all that I am
The thoughts of you racing through my mind

While wondering how this has come to be.
This delight has no name which I can use
Because I am delirious from your magic;
And I will not seek a cure from this
    which happily
    afflicts me.


23


Having met you today and seeing you
    for the first time,
I know that I have finally found someone
With whom I want to share all my life
    never giving up
    this wonderous joy
    of your love.


24


Leaning close you sighed
And I thought for a moment
That my heart had died.


25


I remember so completely calling you
    after a year's absence
    to tell you I had arrived
And how you told me without any hesitation
    that you were waiting
    for me to come to your home.

I cannot forget that first time we ever kissed
    later that afternoon
    when we were together once again.


## 26

Your sensuous lips softly touched mine
    for the first time
Making our long wait just a memory
As we began our new song of love
    for the first time
Knowing there now is only one life for us
    for the first time.


## 27

Croissants, walks, ice cream, talks, laughter,
Holding hands, saying good morning, leaving
Waving at each, returning, letters written,
Calls made, hopes revived, letters read,
And finally together on a lovely voyage
We had waited for all our lives.


## 28

I said a small prayer just for you
Knowing that God would surely hear it;
    giving to you
    joy each day
And happiness in all things you experience
Along with His care for you constantly.

29

Our feelings for each from the first moment
    we ever saw the other
Are like a dandelion losing all its fluff at once
In a delicate breeze dainty and full of desire;
And sometime they are much like a cosmic
Eruption which seems to last forever when
    we now see the other.

30

Why have you come into my life
    in such a strange manner?
To know your name is my wish now;
How can I meet you again
    without stopping to ask
    such a simple question?
Yet I do pass by and must wait again.

Today you spoke to me and I heard more
    than you said as I watched
    your lips move as I smelled
    your fragrance as I wanted
    your soft body this morning.
Come to me again my one of lovely hopes.

31

It was only then in
    the pale light of
    the young evening

that you touched me
And left with my heart.

<br>

## 32

Ecstatically dancing the ancient ceremony
    around amorous flames
    throwing their colorful hues
    on the leaping winds,
Aphrodite touched quickly our hesitant limbs.

Mutually faltering on those simple steps
    we caught one another
    with joyous determination
    as the eveian and adamian
Knowledge forcefully pierced our ignorance.

With hope looking beyond the wondering now
    into the sweepful morrow
    when turbulence gives grace,
    we will still whisper
About that evening of our burning dances.

<br>

## 33

Pale dawn comes to us
As we dream of yesterday's
Ancient calls of love.

34

Finding the moment
When our hearts beat together
Will be happy work.

35

That moment on that enchanting day
When we first met remains fixed
    in my mind
    as something
I never knew could exist between two people.

Something sang loudly that moment to my soul
Urging me to accept the love before me,
    and to forget
    all but you
Who stood silently with hope in your eyes.

That sole moment with you placed in my heart
A feeling I found impossible to resist
    causing me
    to seek more
Of you that enchanting day we first met.

36

We will never decorate as too many others do
    our lover's eyes
    with tears;

And we will never find time as others must
     to fill our lover's ears
     with lies;
Our joy with each will mean constantly that
     our lover's hearts
     will never be wounded.


### 37

Love is a choice
Absent of uncertainty
And truly sublime.


### 38

For a time I was transfixed
     and forgot to wonder
     and peer into the future.
I did not measure how much to give
     by how much I would receive.
That transfixed time I saw only you;
     was it because
     you saw only me?


### 39

We so easily rejoiced that moment of wonder
     when we knew
     each was the person
     of our long dreams.
Having found the other in our searchings

Gave us our own paradise of tranquility
As we began composing our own love song
    in both adoration
    and in thanksgiving
    for the other
    that moment of wonder.

40

It is beyond impossible for me ever to forget
    the moment
    I first
    saw you
Standing there as though you had always been
Waiting for me to arrive in your life.
That small moment of time has been seared into
    my memory
    as nothing
    else ever was
    or ever can be.

41

The moment we saw
Each other that lovely day
We have remembered.

42

Laughter and ice cream on the grounds of the
    old cathedral

Gave us then a glimpse of what could be
If we wanted more of what we found that day
As we walked in discovery and amazement together
    on the grounds
    of the old cathedral.

43

Holding each tightly
So that nothing could enter
Our forever love.

44

The birth of our first child late in the evening
    made so real
    and truly complete
Our deep love we had begun much earlier
In our life which we knew then was lasting.

You so carefully with joy counted each perfect
Finger and toe of our beautiful daughter
Lying quietly on your tired bosom
    as I kissed
    her and you.

We knew then our life together would become
    much richer
    and fulfilling
As we looked in wonder at the tiny miracle
God had given us to cherish that late evening.

## 45

More than we ever
Dreamed of has brought us closer
To each in our lives.

## 46

As though it were yesterday's fond memories,
I can remember so many moments of
     our first times
     so joyfully
     together finally
After days of being with too many other people.

Our first walk alone in the large park caused
Each of us to become giddy with proximity's freedom
     to touch the other
     to hold hands
     to talk openly
As we began our life of wonderous discovery of each.

## 47

A trembling first kiss
Is all that we so desired
That evening of hope.

## 48

Finding you alone
Gave me the needed courage
To give you my love.

## 49

We have no questions or doubts about
    doing again
What we so eagerly wanted when we
    first met.
We wanted to give to the other what
Had been missing for far too long.
Our cherished gift was love, and we became
    united
Without hesitation or discussion of any
Other possibilities we could have known.
We gave then as we would now do again
    our love
    to each.

## 50

In our beginning
When we somehow knew the truth
We became our one.

## 51

I sat lonely apart from all then
    till the moment
    you came to me
And reached out across the blank of my mind
Touching a spirit within me with so very
Careful fingers and strong grasp;
And I looked up to see your lovely smile
Inviting me into your only world.
Words were not needed for a long time
    as we could
    just sit and
Drift in and out of each other's fantasy.
It was all so new to us there.
Yet fresh and with a bitter-sweet tingle.

## 52

Searching for the word
Describing our beginning
Is a lovely task.

## 53

What stirred our summer into flight?
It seemed too hasty and too anxious
    to be gone
    from us
As it scattered clouds and leaves
Moving them far away from us.
Being together for our first time

Caused our summer to flee from us
As though it was jealous of you and me.


54

That constant music you hear daily
Is the sound of my heart beating
    when I see you
    when I hear you
    when I touch you.
That lovely song is within me without
    ceasing
Because you are my only love in my life.


55

I perched lonely on that rock
Frozen on the rim of knowing
    you;
Speaking a word now and then
As I hoped to peer into the future
    of us
Before I heard your singing
    for me
Not a lengthy song of love
But one of our beckoning union.


56

Seeing you alone
More than made up for the crowds
Which had followed us.

## 57

Though you had never seen me before
And had heard very little about me;
When I walked in through your door
    that afternoon,
You told me later that you knew who I was.
You said I must belong to no one but you
And that your love would only be for me.

## 58

Did we ever know that first day of meeting
What could unfold for us as years wore on
    with grace
    with hope
In ways almost mysterious to us now?

As we recall and tell the other our memories
Of that wonderfully enchanting afternoon
    of discovery
    of promise
We have no doubts that we were purposed.

## 59

Words really cannot
Begin to describe my love
To you that first day.

## 60

There is no marveling wonderment that so often
  we want
  to remember
Those beautiful first days of ours from so long ago.
It is for us a retelling of something which seems
To have happened only yesterday and not decades ago.

These memories remain for us so very alive
  in our minds
  in our hearts
That it has become impossible to forget them.
Even if it were possible to remove them from
All that we are for each, it can never be.

## 61

That first time we saw
The other waiting alone
Erased our longings.

## 62

Have you also lost count of the words
  describing our
  first meeting?
Have you also lost count of the memories
  describing our
  first meeting?
Those lost counts are a secure sign for us
That we will never forget those first times
When we knew that the other was the one.

Some things can never escape one's memories
    no matter
    how long ago
Those joyful times were lived so well.
Remembering how we walked along new paths
And how we talked about new topics
    forge completely
    those times
For us as we now easily think of those
    days and nights
    long ago
    yet not so long ago.

Recalling so well
Our first moment together
Is beyond all else.

Did I appear too eager to be only with you
    that first day
When all else receded from my mind
As I saw you that marvelous day?
Or did you think I was much too restrained
    that first day
When I did nothing to indicate my joy?
Or did the others around us notice anything
    that first day
That would give away what we felt so deeply?

## 66

You stopped so easily my running aimlessly
As I attempted to rid myself of cloistered chains
    fastened on me
    by false desires
Which had darkened my life for so long.
Your giving me your gentle heart of love
    chaste and pure
Moved me from my unending moments of doubt
Into your calming sphere of hope and delight
Where I remain in our secure embrace
    now far
    from my past.

## 67

Help me understand this never ending feeling
    of finally belonging
To someone who cares for me without
    reservations of any kind
And who tells me constantly that I am loved.
Where did this true comfort of a lifetime
    come from?
I ask myself and can find no complete answer
To this surrounding aura of wholeness.
Perhaps there is no answer because it is.

## 68

How did you appear
That momentous day of love
When I was alone?

## 69

At first I could not
Believe the overwhelming
Beauty of your love.

## 70

Exploding in my mind that first day
    of our discovery
Was the imaging of how my life would have been
    so very different
Had we not from those faraway lands met
Almost by chance in another country that
    magical day
When with profound joy we accepted one another.

## 71

When you came to me with golden words
    so strange to me
Who had heard only blackened and unruly
Words from those before your coming into
    my disordered life,
I knew I viewed perfection not a vision.
I remember embracing all that you so gladly
Offered me in my tremulous unkept state
    and desiring that this
    so welcomed difference
    would never vanish.

## 72

Before I saw you
That afternoon of surprise
I was so empty.

## 73

How could we know that our first day
Would lead to many years of deep joy
    for each to savor
    and hold dearly
As we gained momentum from our surprised start?

We have searched in vain for some answers,
But have never found any which would show
    others how we
    were able to live
With growing love through all these years.

## 74

Our love from the beginning of our great
    journey together
Created for each of us kindness which we
    had not known before.
We learned to give not with any expectation
Of anything given in return from the other,
But rather because giving is right.
What most can never learn is that giving
Is never wasted and can never be lost.

## 75

Finding each other
That glorious and good time
Gave us a new life.

## 76

That very moment of first seeing you has been
     seared into
     my eternal soul
Beyond my futile attempts of description for that moment
When all of time collapsed around me standing there
Hoping that what was would never not be.
My feelings of being vulnerable and alone vanished
     without effort
As I felt for the first time ever made new.
Calling to memory now is remembering how
We two became one that first moment.

## 77

Did my soul know then
Before my head and heart did
That we had found love?

## 78

Loving you with all my heart;
Holding you with all my strength;
Needing you with all my mind;

Keeping you with all my soul
Are my ways of knowing that love
    is an infinite journey;
And that nothing will take me farther than
    our journey of love.


## 79

Being loved is a lesson which seldom comes
    easily for us,
But learning it well always changes those
Who understand that earning rather than accepting
    can never
    be the way
No matter how hard we may try to make sure
    we are loved.
Being loved is not about how good one is,
But it must be rooted in the incomparable
Goodness of a love which fills us with
    awe
And sends us running to spend time with
    the one
    who loves us.


## 80

Finding you that day
Removed all those memories
From my barren past.

# 81

My dimmed vision was at once broadened
When I at last found you who saw
Somehow in my darkened self a person
    who would
    seek love
    with you.
Who was I to expect anyone to see in me
A person who would forget his uneven life
And gain insight from merely being with you?
I was forcefully reminded that though I saw
    dimly through
    a broken mirror,
My visual field of life would always be enhanced
    by you
    and your love
    for me.

# 82

Hold me now with your
Love which I had never known
Before I met you.

# 83

Participating
Now in your glorious love
Is all that I need.

## 84

Love lies constantly at the heart of all we do;
Nothing matters in the end without whole love
Which not only gives us a joyous love
But also guides and protects us each day.
     Without love
     We are nothing.
Nothing can matter in our lives but to love
And to know completely that we are loved.
     Not having love
     We have nothing.


## 85

That profound message
Revealing completely to us
Our love shines brightly.


## 86

We will be rewarded in ways we cannot begin now
     to imagine
As we so willingly give to the other our gifts
Which appear joyfully to number those of the stars
As they look upon the beginning of our togetherness.
We will learn from each other what the other
     may lack
And find rest and peace as we align our hopes.
We understand there will be struggles in our life,

But we also know so well that the other
     will always help
     carry the other's
     unnamed burden.

87

Finding each was right
As our prior worlds never
Gave us this joy.

88

Beyond all my dreams
You opened wide my closed door
To a life of love.

89

Before knowing or even being aware of the other
     we were never whole beings
As we searched for what we knew we lacked
     to fill our emptiness
Which had been created by our separation;
And now that we are finally together as meant,
We can live as whole beings brought together by love.

## 90

Coming to your peaceful shore through those
   turbulent seas
   of my past
Provided at once all that I had never before known.
Only in my momentary dreams could I have imagined
What a solid life could be free from imposed wills
   as I struggled
   to see clearly
Those far vistas of peace, joy, and love
Which you offered to me without conditional questions.

## 91

Those eager good days
Were our joyous beginnings
Of love and laughter.

## 92

Holding you so close
Has given me the freedom
I had so longed for.

## 93

Moving from my disorded life of non-love
To your calm life of open love for me
Amazed those who thought they knew me well.
   Why the wonderment

And even questions
Of my reasoning?
You accepted me with all my past burdens
Without wonderment or questions from you
As we became one in the midst of all that then was.

94

Accepting me then
Was the most wonderful thing
That ever happened.

95

We had no doubts that day of our
        first meeting,
Even as we had no knowledge of the other,
That we had somehow already known
So very well the other when we first met
        that late summer
        afternoon of discovery.
There was nothing strange or odd as we
Sat in your crowded flat among those
Who knew us and began our first never
        hesitant talk.
You knew as I also knew that much more
Would envelope us that day of our
        first meeting.

96

Being next to you
That very first time ever
Was all I desired.

97

What were you thinking
That afternoon standing there
Seeing me alone?

98

Memories are sound
When they recall our first time
We saw the other.

99

Why were we so reluctant to admit that day
    that each
    was so attracted
    to the other?
What kept our mouths closed to what our minds
Were feverishly expressing when we first met?
How was it possible that each was able
    to remain
    so pregnantly
    silent then?
When did we know that the other was thinking

The same thoughts as the other was?
Perhaps our mutual silence came because
      we somehow knew
      that much more
      would come to us.


                    100


Our very first kiss
Held us in a rapture not
Known by us before.


                    101


We have never found it strange or
Even odd as some have told us repeatedly
      that we can
      recall exactly
What transpired that day of our lovely firsts.
How can we forget what each had never had
      before seeing
      the other?
We have always told those who almost do not
Believe us that we have memories they
      should have
      also had.


                    102


Your great gift to me
Was accepting me as I was
And not as you hoped.

## 103

Our remembering our first fragile moments
Of long ago has always cancelled any attempts
By anyone or anything at forgetting what happened
During those epiphanies we eagerly encountered
 in a country
 not yours
 nor mine.
There can never be for us a putting aside of
The truthful and obvious movements toward a knowing
Of who each was and what could be for us
As we began to sense the great need of the other
 to be united
 as we grew
 slowly together.

## 104

With tentative hope
We approached each other then
Not knowing our way.

## 105

Buying you for the first time anything
Stirred my thoughts as nothing before;
Even though what I gave you that afternoon
In the cathedral's park was only an ice cream.
 You received it
 As I gave it
 With pure joy
 Seen in our faces.

## 106

Never expecting
More than polite greetings then
Was not what happened.

## 107

Those ten days or so before I had to leave
The country where we first met will assuredly
Come only once to a fortunate few
Who are blessed as we were then.
We must hope for them that they will recognize
    what we saw
    at once
    when we met.
More than seeing, we knew then clearly
That much more than a chance encounter
Was involved and directing us firmly
Toward a lifetime of joyous exploration
Which has continued without ceasing
    as we know
    those ten days
    were meant for us.

## 108

You told me later
That you already knew me
When at first we met.

# 109

We remain enthralled even now decades later
By those first few days when we met
And slowly began to know one another.
We were careful not to reveal what our feelings were
Even though those who knew us saw
    how inseparatable
    we so quickly became.
We knew the bond was there, and there deeply,
But we did not want to do anything which
Might cause the other to doubt any sincerity.
Even what we said was so very circumspect
Without any hints which would indicate
    how inseparatable
    we so quickly became.

# 110

Going with you there
I would not have done alone
Has opened my eyes.

# 111

Holding me so close
Gave me that precious short day
Visions of more days.

## 112

Never wavering in our hope as we waited
    so very impatiently
    for long months
To know and see whom we had longed for;
We somehow realized that this birth
Would not only be an amazing event for us
But also that it would alter in the best manner
What our lives would then become.
We carried a sense of gratitude that enabled
    us to accept
    what would be
No matter what we desired in our daily talks.

When that truly momentous morning arrived,
We heard and received the overwhelming news
That the birth of our second child was indeed
What we had hoped for all those preceding months.
The amazing gift of a son completed what
We had long hoped for our small family.

# II
## Melodies

1

My body is like a melody,
And yours like a word on it
    making a lovely song
    that sings without stopping.

2

You and I
    are common lips
    singing the best
    of love songs.
You and I
    are common eyes
    seeing the world
    together in our lives.
You and I
    are common passions
    better than all the flames
    burning before us.

3

Whenever you fall
I will forever catch you
With my heart and arms.

## 4

They said the angels sang that day;
 they said
The heavens shone brilliantly that day;
 they said
The supplies of elegance were diminished that day;
 they said
There was no more beauty left that day;
 they said
My heart rejoiced as never before that day
When me love came into my life.

## 5

You have lifted me higher
Than I ever
 thought possible;
You have embraced me with more love
Than I ever
 thought possible;
You have given me more hope
Than I ever
 thought possible;
Without you I would have remained
Incomplete.

## 6

As though you were I,
 you made me
 more with your self

Until we were one.
And you will be with me
     in the safest place
That one can find;
You will always be
     in my heart.

7

I awaken to watch you sleeping
     next to me;
I awaken to wait for you to awaken
     next to me;
I awaken to want to touch your body
     next to me;
I awaken to know that you have
     given me
     so much more
Than I could ever have thought possible;
And I realize so fully that I must
     hold closely
     each moment
As the fragile jewel it is.

8

You have become more than my lover;
     you have made me
     part of a metamorphosis
     reflecting more
Than dreams could create in a thousand nights.
You are

A prism
    tossing hued joys of living
    into my prison
Where I had etched on the hard walls
Each attempt of escape into those spaces
    I could only see dimly.


9


Your name whispered is like
    a sharp barb catching
    on my heart
    and tearing it.
But I welcome this tearing
    as I welcome
    the warmth of
    the sun on a
    cold winter day
For it promises hope and life.


10


To see and not hear you
    is not enough;
To hear and not touch you
    is not enough;
To touch and not hold you
    is not enough;
To hold and not kiss you
    is not enough;
To kiss and not love you
    is not enough;

To love and not keep you
   is not enough;
.

What have you and all the gods
   of love
   done to me?


## 11


Let us then for each make the best
   love song
While our moment of knowing is suspended,
   and though consumed
   to be returned,
As we find a beginning of ever growth.

You are the breezes blowing over me
Scattering everywhere my fragrances
   of love
   and desire
Causing each now to find a silent urge to say
Our hearts have become the other's life;
And we can breathe with no fear
As we each understand that we
   have become
   the blooms
   of all our seasons.


## 12


Give me new your soft hand
   and kind heart

And let us be together here and tomorrow
Knowing that nothing can separate us
As we leave behind with full love
    my sorrowing heart
Finding from each those dreams now
Making firmly real our long desires
    for all beyonds.


## 13


We are now here thinking no more
    of lost yesterdays
As our dreams are now become real
Finding in the other care that had never
Been part of our lives lived apart.

We are surrounded this wonderful day
    by our memories
Made from knowing how love is always
Attentive to the other and gives in a manner
The other most needs in our new life.

We are kept secure because we understand
    love offers freely
With no conditions ever put on its giving
Abundantly without asking the other
What needs may someday be required.


## 14


You held me as I had never been held
    before

Because you sensed in me a need long
    neglected.
You wrapped your kind arms around me
Without knowing the cause of my need,
And told me without any hesitation
That you would always hold me.

I never asked how you knew so well
What I needed in those hard days.
I knew only that you were always
With me when I had nothing.
Even now those memories keep me
    after
You told me what you deeply knew I
    needed.


15


When I called you that day of no
    hotel rooms
    or any place
    to rest;
And you said I could stay with you,
I landed on your doorstep thinking
    only of sleep.
My being there in front of you caught
    both of us
    totally unawares
    of other needs
As we later found each so impossible to resist.

16

My only love came into my life
    like a perfect ballet
    with enchanting music
Sounding throughout my empty heart
Until every part of my body danced
    in harmony
    with yours.


17

At first so dimly lighted were our
    beings
That each was afraid to reach
And touch the other.
It was as though all we knew
    was so full
    of unknowns
That we were unable to see what
Was sparkling and only stood still
Waiting for love to shine brightly
    in our hearts.


18

Sitting here alone, again, in my hotel room,
I can think only of the glorious days
    spent with you
As we began our moments of learning
What the other thought of so many things.

I want to capture just a part of our
Time together in a few poems for you
    to read and remember
Where we were and what we did
Together those far too few times we saw the other.

I will write of our long walk that evening
When we were so overly careful not to hold
    even our hands
On that enchanted walk back to your flat
Where people were asking where we were.

I will also write of our moment on the
Ruined tower that afternoon when I told you
    not to fall
And that I would hold you if you
Misplaced your feet on the old stairs.

I will copy each poem carefully
After I have written them and then post
    them to you
So that you will receive them after
I leave tomorrow with you on my mind.

19

My arms are no longer empty
Because you are in them
    for the rest
    of my life.
My life is no longer empty
Because you are in it
    for the rest
    of our life.

20

There can be no explaining from anyone
How your warmth has infused into me
    much more
Than I could ever have dreamed of
    or desired;
And with no explanation, I gladly live
With only you next to me as we give
    openly to each
      pleasure and happiness.


21

How is it possible that your glowing smile
    enchants me now
    more than when
    we first met,
And your full love for me exceeds
What was in our beginning long ago?
Our devotion to one another is perhaps
One reason I feel as though we have
    just met
    and are
Now starting our always together life.


22

Come to me if your heart is empty of love
    and stay with me
While I fill your lonely heart with ancient
    songs of love and hope

Which will remain with you forever.

Come to me if your life is empty of joy
     and stay with me
While I fill your empty life with glorious
     days of joy and wonder
Which will never leave you in our togetherness.

Come to me;
Stay with me.


### 23

Our story of love became complete when we
     first saw our
     creation from that
     consuming love of ours,
And heard those joyous cries of life from
Our child late that summer evening.
We were made stronger that exquisite moment
For we were together then as a family
     knowing this baby
     was a lovely
     part of each of us
Made into one sublime person for our happiness.


### 24

Love always directs to look beyond now
     and leads us
Away from here to another world where we
     can share

All that we each are with the other.

How do we listen to our hearts knowing
    there are many
Voices calling to us throughout all our days
    speaking loudly
Against our love which changes all things?

We listen carefully since we know well
    the depth of our love
Which leads us with purpose beyond our now.


25

Your manner of dress
More than charms me
    as you know
When I see you now.


26

From you I have refound hope
And have learned again of love
    hidden so long
    under my loneliness
Where shadows always grow heavy.

Your laughter came dancing to me
As a flame piercing those shadows
    revealing me
    to myself
When I was lost and all alone.

Those lovely necklaces of your laughter
Hang around our days together
    sparkling with
    ever new joys
On this new and endless river of hope.


## 27

When my heart and mind run to you,
    my only one,
I am running to myself as the spring winds.
For the first time I see an emptiness in my being,
    and now I need
    that other part
Or else I can never be complete.
Let us take strength from this life
We now have and create a hope beyond
    all dreams
    for each.
And then let us together realize that hope,
    my only one.


## 28

Lingering with you
Is like racing the new day
Through the lovely night.

## 29

All that I can be
Comes from your wonderful love
You give just to me.

## 30

Gently you have caught me
    with your
    silken glances,
And now I have no more voiceless questions
    racing through
    my mind
As I did before your full capture of me.

## 31

Those soft yet urgently warm embraces
    on our September
    night of desire
Are those moments which we can never
Forget even if we were told to forget them.
They remain with us as though they happened
    last night
    instead of
Decades ago in our forever united life.

## 32

Slow but ever sure for us
Came the flaming moment
When we knew our lives
Would be joined in love
    until all
    time ceases.

## 33

Our overwhelming feeling for each did not arrive
    unannounced.
For we found in the other the cherished gift
We each had been seeking long before we met.
United by love we became as one whole
For the best of all possibly given reasons:
    You are mine;
    I am yours.

## 34

I can never have enough of seeing my only you
    in the morning
    during the day
    in the evening
As we open widely the doors of our beings to the other
Giving without ever realizing we gave freely all
We have to each with no wish to receive anything
    ever in return.

## 35

Sing with me that song
Which sounds of our happiness
Each day of our life.

## 36

You told me in your card I read eagerly today
That you would always be grateful that you
    found me
    and I would
    always be yours
    forever.
The happiness I felt when I read your words
Left me feeling as though I could not possibly
    want anything
    more than
    what you meant.

## 37

More than bright cherry blossoms every spring
And always more than festive autumn leaves
Is our bubbling joy with one another
    through all seasons
Because our love rekindles daily for each
Without having to wait for an approaching season
    to decorate
    what we have.

## 38

The bells of the church
Were pealing our full union
As we became one.

## 39

When I awake in the morning and see
    your beautiful face
I become then more blessed than anyone
Can possibly imagine or be on this earth.
You give me without trying my reason
    to live
    in love
No matter what events of the new day
May attempt to move my from my joy.

## 40

Being together brings
Happiness far beyond what
Most can ever know.

## 41

Thinking of you and how we enjoy each other
Is truly one of life's great features for me
In the midst of all that is wrong in the world
    where so few
    can live in

peace and quiet
As you and I so easily do every day.
Our harmonious togetherness creates for us
    an oasis
Where we are refuged from the din of chaos.


42


Moments linger now
And grow into more moments
Of forever love.


43


Let us whisper in the dark when our
    light is dim
And when we need the peace of always
    feeling wanted
As the world vainly attempts to part us.

Let us whisper in the dark when we need
    to make
The other know that our committed love will make
    the other stronger
Even as we hear doubts from outside.

Let us whisper in the dark what our hearts
    tell us
When we need to hear that our love is
    a choice
We would make again as in our beginning.

## 44

Sing our song of love
During the day as we walk
Always together.

## 45

When you told me you were finally returning
    to our home
    to my arms
Without any further delays keeping us apart
    so far away,
My heart began joyously bursting with more
Happiness than I had known for a long time
As I realized that we would be together
    as we had
    always wanted.

## 46

Finally coming home
After far too many weeks
Gives us renewed hope.

## 47

Returning at last
To your home and only love
Where all our joy is.

## 48

Seeing your kind face
Removes all the lonely time
We were so apart.

## 49

The nights are finally peaceful here
 alive and hung
Along some silk smooth thread of destiny's love
Bordered around by stars which seem as
 close and lively
As the fireflies which seek in circles bright
To find the darkening homeward path.

The days are finally shining as shields
 clear and burnished
Along their even rows protecting one's love
From distant wars which only now and then
 guiltily rumble
Across the demanding stillborn air as
Those rising muses love-slain appear.

## 50

As I openly sing a taut, gentle, savage
Or grieving song to you and only to you,
It must never be a lengthy song;
Or I will certainly lose my voice
 of love.

## 51

Transfixed by the first dawn in a
Hundred years of night with only restless
    dreams,
Lovers promise each again that new
Bridges would be built to last.
Finding their way through strange
Territories and unseen egos lurking
    in the canyons
    of their souls,
Lovers rejoin with new hope for a future
Filled with all that had never been.


## 52

Into the far reaches of known eternity
With stunning promises beyond telling
    rise
The wonders of love not yet ours to know.
These joyous apparitions must change us
    as we live
In the way we love here on this earth.


## 53

There are no restrictions in our affections
As we without effort keep wide our hearts
Rather than closing them to keep them safe
    from harm.
We understand well that it is always difficult
To be willing to be openly vulnerable to each;

The only true way we can fully love one another
Is to keep our hearts wide open so that
    we may sing
    loudly to our souls.


54


Walking now quickly
We cannot now wait to be
In the other's arms.


55


There is no reason why lovers want to give
Their abilities to love each with their whole hearts;
It remains a sublime and fulfilling experience
Which gives always to the other deeply loved one
    a paradise
    on earth
Where there coexists a pleasure of discovery
Through the desire to care for each other with
    thankfulness
    each day,
And those lovers will always know that being
Loved gives more courage than can be dreamed of.


56


As we viewed all of London from the top
    of the hill
    we climbed

On our late summer walk on that shady
Path near the river with fragrant flowers
Welcoming us on our slow walk along
The narrow lane filled with deep greenery,
We were aware of the promises we each
    would give
    on the walk
    through our life.


## 57

What have we heard this young day
As we awaken next to one another?
Have we heard what all lovers desire to hear
    as a new
    day arrives?
The easily given words of devotion to the other
Fills the hearts of both with pleasure never
    found anywhere
    anytime else.
The freely given pleasure of spoken words
Becomes the secure beginning of another day.


## 58

Catullus was right –
Let us live and love today
And rejoice in each.

59

Freedom at last
Greets us daily in our lives
As we live with love.

60

Awaiting the lover's thirst will always be
    the wine
    from the summer's
    ripe fruit
Made into the drink which slackens the desire
For more than can be offered.
Loving the giver more than one's self creates
    a fullness
    and wholeness
As each accepts that the all is in the other.

61

The barely discernible harbor lights in the heavy fog
    of the morning
Twinkle with a beckoning as they reach beyond
Their prison of enshrouding greyness which they
    did not create.
This attempt to be what they were created for
In spite of the apparent burden forces a feeling
    of wholeness
Much as love will when pressed by less than
What it also was created for.

## 62

When we understand that love will always
    be more than
    only words,
And when we give to the other freely what
    we do know
    is needed;
Then we realize fully there is a rather fine line
    between
Doing something well and doing something well
    only for recognition.

## 63

From the heights of lovers' created memories
Falling as streakingly bright meteors toward
    a waiting earth
Come the cascading cries of shared joys
Which only they can possess and consume
    unknown to others.
These moments are never meant to be rare
Since they are always reformed newly for those who
    accept tomorrow.

## 64

Never ending want
Pursues all lovers daily
Without any end.

## 65

We have all been strangers in need of love
    and kindness
    just as children
In their innocent cries for our attention.
We must remember the last time the one
Whom we say we love and care for
Needed us when that one reached out to us.
Do you remember the one who showed you
    love and kindness
    without your
    ever asking?

## 66

Holding each tightly
Creates a lovely moment
For us to repeat.

## 67

When hard days bring unfortunate tears,
Let us consider that wind, rain, and whispers
    will always
    encourage us
To forget the difficult moment which caused
Each to move from what we are to each;
And then to rekindle our hearts as we
    remember well
That we must love the other more than our self.

Hearing your kind voice
Reminds me of our joyful
Years spent together.

Do lovers in their wanted reluctance to be
    vulnerable
And to keep silent about their long needs
Understand that this hardness of heart is far
    more crippling
To any union than any physical limitation?
Love shines brightly in the midst of our
Brokenness and determination to be difficult.
Lovers should remember that the emptying
    of self
Is doing the right thing for the right reason.

This world where we learn to love is always
The world where we are with no escaping into
Any unprotected place where temptations have
    not yet found
    pure hearts;
Solitude can never be any answer for those
Who find the need to flourish in love far
From those delirious and boundless thoughts
Proclaiming that deeds are the only evil visited
On any union secured in light not darkness.

Love will never be the power of resistance;
It can truthfully be only the loyalty of faithfulness.


71


Loving you is all
I can ever desire now
And all I can need.


72


Telling our story of love from our hearts
Really is not magical or extraordinary;
We know that this song has changed our lives
    where all are
    welcomed and celebrated.
We refuse to run from hurt or humiliation
As we run toward all who see us and
    who want to know
    how we built
    this tower of strength.


73


Laughing and always
Eager to see each other
Has been our good life.

## 74

While carrying pain that is raw and real,
Showing compassion in the face of all wants
Helps us remember that loving another is
     perhaps
     the only way
That wrongs can be forgiven no matter how uncomfortable.
Remembering that most people are fortunate
To get away with their dissatisfactions most of the time
Helps us to understand profoundly that all
     love is a
     tender mercy.

## 75

Though there have been uncertainties along
Our journey of love with perhaps more to come,
This wanting to be known and loved by each
     set our lives
     on a new trajectory
Which has been both stunning and staggering.
We do tell each other frequently that our
Acceptance of this has become the purpose
     of our lives
Giving us joy in our search for committed love.

## 76

Understanding impossible moments intruding
In our lives causing us to feel confused
     at the way
     our world

Has been reorganized will constantly help us
To have our eyes opened and our hearts softened
When we accept that our yesterdays are never
Lost if we are utterly astounded by perceptions
     of why
     and how
By remembering that we should not push away
The answers to the why or the questions about the how.


## 77

Thoughts of our joy
Come flooding to us daily
Giving us more love.


## 78

Loving each into wholeness and truth
     will create miracles
Which we could not have known
With our blind spots causing us to see
     only in part
Before we knew we could not travel our
     journey alone.
When we judge with pity or compassion,
We really do see our errors reflected
     in the face of the other;
So despite our lack of compassion sometime,
We remain the same person we have so
     harshly judged
Until we open up to the possibilities to live
Beyond our own self interest into trust.

We should live as if love is profoundly,
Completely, and concretely true; we should
Long to be kind, tender hearted, and forgiving
    while imagining
    what life
    would look like
If we each believed we were totally loved and accepted.
We often admit that it is far easier to remain
Apart from what love may call us to be and do;
And would somehow prefer great losses
    in our finite
    understanding
    of love
Than to accept that love is a precious and infinite
    gift of life.

80

Walking together
Always brings more happiness
To those who want it.

81

Something which could be for each of us both
    mistakable and miraculous
Should never frighten us but give us freedom
To let go of our certainty about how we think
    things should be.
Being comfortable and leaving what we know

To go to a place in our lives we cannot imagine
Will lead us with the comfort that we are
Never alone in this journey to unknown places.
Just because we do not know where we are going
Does not mean we are not being led
    to a place
    we cannot imagine.


## 82

Regardless of where we may be in life
With its challenges physically, mentally, or spiritually,
The possession of joyful love will speak much
    louder
Than any questions we may have about our worth.
We will know that this truth of love will invite
    us openly;
And we will know that we are home and safe
With doubts fully erased and replaced by peace.


## 83

What do we need to let go of however
    big or small
Which keeps us from running full tilt
Into the holy place of secure love?
Walking in the freedom which love and integrity
Will give us gladly is an opportunity
    to choose
    to live
Intentionally and explicitly with hope and joy
We may never have considered before.

## 84

Brightly shining new
Is your forever promise
Of loving just me.

## 85

Opening up ourselves without hesitation to
    the reality
Of a dynamic and life-changing union
With someone who loves us and whom we love
Gives each the mystical ability to participate
Actively in the renewal of all things important
    including our
    broken hearts
    and shattered selves
With astounding clarity and gracious mercy.

## 86

When we accept love without doubts or questions,
There will be for us who do not turn aside
    this offer
A definitive moment of transformation of all
    we are;
This acquiring moment appears only because
We have a willingness to hold mercy and grace
As that determination of love which will go
    far beyond
Our thoughts of harboring any foolish reluctance
As we truly open our closed selves to wonder.

## 87

Do we wonder as we ought without taking
    for granted
That a simple sunrise can never be just
Like any other time of our given days?
As the pitch dark gives way to another
Glorious sunrise beckoning all to enjoy
The peaceful morning hush before any
Demands intrude on us to tarnish this newness
Offering us moments filled with hope and love,
It just might be the reason for each new day
    precisely so that
    we could be reminded
    of hope and love.


## 88

In our ignorance we too often feel compelled
    to choose
Only because we know that not choosing is also
    a choice.
Being open to a new direction eliminates that
Question which becomes a struggle when we
Are fearful of sharing what we realize is
The goodness of love which frees all from
Malice and folly and injury when we refuse
To see the gleaming and overpowering beauty
    in the giving
    of our love
Which brings healing and joy with a free choice
Relieving our restless thoughts of not choosing
    to share always
    the grace of love.

## 89

When our lives are love-filled with deep
    care and concern
For each other in this restless world of want,
We will be laying a solid foundation which
    will be beneficial
    for others
As we simply take the time to assess
Where we are in any area of living today.
If we pause and consider whether the path
We are on is free of all harm to others,
We will come to know the great joy
    of love given
    to those
    we know.

## 90

Hearing your voice
Always fills me with joy
In the midst of life.

## 91

Those mysteries of ancient times which we
    often cannot
    see or understand
Tell us a deeper truth with their holy grace
Far exceeding our human standards of fairness.
When we recognize these mysteries of long ago,
We will recognize the almost invisible line

between goodness
and wrongness;
And then we are able to offer help with joy
To those who most need what we can give.


## 92


Happiness is here
With us every awesome day
As we walk our path.


## 93


As our confusion with somber choices dim wishes,
We can more easily listen intently
To those sounds of wholeness which we had
    earlier not heard
    in our deafness.
We will be able to feel the rhythm of creation
When we let go of our fixed feelings and then
We can peer out our formerly clouded window
And hear well with solid contemplation those
    forgotten and muted
    cries of new living.


## 94


Let us sing that ancient song of mercy and justice,
And extol those great virtues together constantly.
Let us freely choose restorative rather than retributive
    justice and mercy

On our far too short walk in this life of choice.
Let us always remember with considered thought
That true justice need not be blind as some say.
Let us also rejoice in the impact of knowing
That mercy is the better part of justice.
We can then see life in its fullness as we
    defy the usual
    and cultivate an
    enduring vitality.


95


Joyous is our love
And enduring for all time
In our surrender.


96


Whatever our lack or whatever our loss
As we plunge through our personal valleys,
Whether we have or do not have hard burdens;
We each have the ability to choose love
    and the gracious
    attitude which comes
    from and through love.
We really can love with all our heart, mind, and soul
Those who appear unlovable in our lives.
There is no secret knowledge or insider privilege,
And regardless of rank, station, or status;
We can truly and freely offer without exception
    to anyone
    our love.

## 97

A great cosmic song is sung with full voice
Resounding always throughout the holy universe
Vibrating forth from all created atoms
    unceasingly
    and eternally
Even in the most isolated place and desolate state
Joined by choirs visible and invisible
Making an eternal song as invocation and praise
For the wonders of whole love.

## 98

Things too wonderful
Which neither of us could know
Have now made us whole.

## 99

When you have been made painfully enlightened
And a heretofore unexplored world has opened
    to your limited perspective,
You will realize that vistas never seen before
Await your avid discovery each day
As you ask yourself why you waited so long
Even though your fear of seeing prevented you
    from seeking
    more to learn.

## 100

Hearing now those sounds
Of our voices this morning
Reminds us of love.

## 101

Your presence so transforms all who see you
        that wonder and reflection
        in their bold claims
        and manifold meanings
Evoke even more perplexity because of the depth
        of your presence
        with its generosity.
This power and strength you have so abundantly
Creates an unwavering trust which provides
Relief from trials and resolutions of crises and
        consolation of desolation
With the miracle that there is always more.

## 102

Your always bright smile
Welcomes me into your life
With such graciousness.

## 103

Life-changing love and whole compassion
        to others

When our own stresses, relationships, and obligations
Threaten to pull us down from what we are
Are those great things in life which allows us
    to see
However briefly that burdens must be shared
And simple pleas for help must be answered.


## 104

Ringing so brightly
Are the sounds of your laughter
Removing from me doubt.


## 105

Do we really always understand those wonderful
Questions asked of us by those who love us
    as they ask
    simple questions?
Keeping visible the answers never fragmented
By dishonesty becomes our challenge when we allow
    deeply personal
    confessions shape
Every aspect of our lives from the depths of our love
As we give abundantly without the sake of sacrifice.


## 106

Only hearing you
Lightens my daily burden
As I now listen.

## 107

Moving from the darkness of only self
And on to removing anxieties which cannot teach;
One finds that irritations are so very minor
    when compared
    to a gracious life
When one quickly comes to know that love
And the joy which follow are the true source
    of the reality
    of our humanity.

## 108

Seeing only you
Is all I will ever need
Now that we have met.

## 109

Running with you and knowing your laughter
Brightens the dreariest day so easily
That I often forget what my life was like
    before you entered
    and remained in
    my former self.
It has now become wholly impossible
To imagine a time when your joy did not
Inhabit my previous empty being.
Without effort you lighten all my moments
    with your grace
    and wonderful charm
    so freely given to me.

## 110

Thoughts of only you
Gives me the necessary strength
To continue living.

## 111

How the memories flooded my eager mind
As I watched you walk on the beach moving
So elegantly even though all you were doing
Was looking for sea shells and your
Prized and rare sea fans which you carefully
Brought home and framed so very well.
I waited until you had almost receded from sight
    before I began
    running after you
    wanting so deeply
    to know what
    you were thinking
As you gathered the lovely sea shells and a sea fan.

## 112

Happiness cannot
Completely describe for all
What we have in each.

## 113

Awakening each morning with you next to me
Is a moment I want to cherish always
Because the sense of purpose it imparts
Cannot be found anywhere else in my day.
Watching you as you become aware
    of me
    next to you
Are those parcels of time which easily magnify
My devotion to the one who accepted me both
    with my faults
    and my strengths.

## 114

Holding you is all
I can now desire for me
As we awaken.

## 115

You saw me in the crowded room that day
    looking for you
    as though I was
    searching for a
    lost precious jewel
Which without I would have been less than whole.
You told me later that the others in that room
Had expressions both of surprise and knowing
When they saw me rushing toward you
And finally jumping over a chair to be next to you.

All I remember of those moments of decision
Is that I finally saw you and had to be
    next to the one
    who had so
    thoroughly captured
    all of my being.


116


Talking while walking
With you as my companion
Must be what God meant.


117


Seeing you sitting on the bench in seeming deep thought
Caused me to hope that you might be thinking of us
And how much we already meant to the other
So soon after our mutual and chance meeting
    which quickly opened
    our hearts widely
    for each to explore.


118


Laughing and talking
Now as though we had just met
Pervades our good life.

# 119

You called me early this morning with love
    from far away
To wish me a happy birthday and told me how
You wanted to be with me today.
After all our years together, I still
    remain surprised
By your caring devotion to me.
You are so constant and strong in everything
That I thank God daily for your presence in my life.
Today I realize once again with clarity
How very much you have so gently
    changed my life.

# 120

Knowing you are here
Enthralls me every moment
As I breathe freely.

# 121

Helping you with the small matters of life
    truly lifts me
Beyond considering them mundane or small
To a knowledge that, if I did not do them,
I would be far less than a person who has said
That what I do for you will always be far less
    than what you
    have given me.

## 122

Rushing through my mind
Are those joyous thoughts of you
Surrounding my soul.

## 123

Your place in my life
Gives me every day such hope
That I am at peace.

## 124

We did not know when you and I began
Flipping large acorns across the driveway
Of your school while waiting for your sister
After I picked you up from your pre-school
That the simple action of doing what we did
With those acorns would quickly lead to
Your learning how to count in a foreign language.

 Counting while playing
 Was then an effortless way
 To use our good time together.

Memories such as those never haunt us
But rather provide a firm bridge from now
  back to then
  when all was
  so much simpler.

# III
## Symphonies

1

Can lovers ever recognize or ever know
    when each gives
All to the other in everything every day;
Or do some say it does not matter
    when one gets
    and the other does not?
When time moves through the lives
    of lovers
    and uncovers frailties,
Those who both give to each their all
Will find that loving and living
    became equal.



2

Is there a never-ending cycle of living
    and feeling
    and knowing
What we experience on our samsaras?
Perhaps any answers are well-hidden
    except for those
    who seek
Wanting to love fully the other.
How else can it be explained clearly
That detailed want of
    are you still mine
Or the equally deep from the heart of
    wait for me?
As lovers hunger for the touch of each,
So must they search
    for the food

Which will satisfy what each
     lacks
     from the other.


                    3


Lying next to me breathing
     now softly
In our tousled bed of love,
I attempt to find a time
     when I began
     loving you.
There was no beginning of our love;
     it came to us
As we were searching for much more
Than short moments with others
     as we were
     wanting much more.
We now share our love as love
     must be shared
Between those who want a fullness
In their lives together
     in a world
     where fullness is rare.


                    4


It will always seem to others
     who see us
     and think they know us
     that we are foolish;

What they can never see or know
　　is a binding
　　we have
Which is much stronger than
　　all the doubts
　　ever put together
　　against us.


5


We know our mornings came far
　　too fast
Against hope for a few more hours
As we desire moments which enlighten
　　us
By fusing doubts into beliefs
　　for both
As we each find common joy
Letting
　　our autumn of love
Be the first
　　summer of our life.


6


When we find that our walk
　　with new discoveries
Has slowed to a trying crawl,
It is then that we will find
　　more strength
　　more love
　　more hope

Than we ever believed possible
By our calm telling to each
What the other already deeply
    knew.


7


What is it faintly down sounding through
    your longings freely
    as you reach with
    racing thoughts toward
Afternoon rooms ardor fragranced and rain cooled
Rhymed forever with urgent meters?

Do ghostly arms too real encircle you
Or do dream arms embrace a fevered body?
Old love-stained beds need not have
    winding sheets
    which enshroud today
And all your imagined tomorrows
With hopes beyond all your necessities.


8


Running there where I had been
    so deep and lost
    in stagnant pools reflecting
    lust for self,
You broke boldly my mirror
    and carefully placed
    each fragment under
    the pestle of love

And ground carefully and surely
    until only the dust
    of a thousand prideful dreams
    glittered genesisily
Yielding laughing joys to be soon
    edened by your hands
    into bare life
    together and together always.


9


There can be no forced end of our
    togetherness
As we become newly born from our
    memories
    of our
    young yesterdays
Knowing that the other also moves from
The fogs of fear into non-demanding brilliant
Lightning reminding leading with places
And thoughts never to be forgotten.

It is not that we have died to our
    now selves;
It is that we recount with ever increasing
    number
Those times which created our full beings.
We find fully that without this elemental
Feeling of each with experienced love
Can we realize with a quickening realization
That our names are the only names we
    want to know
    always.

## 10

Mounting easter orb fuiji flung moves slowly
    newfoundlandward eventually and without fail
    to uncover again
What had been moon shrouded evenly
In its remembered absence.

Defying thermometers and other measurements
And flare filled beyond need in joyous
    dances,
This one cannot be caught, taught, or
Scorned by mediocrity worshipping rabble.

Torched into brilliance by cause before
    man was adamed
    and placed punctiliously perfect
For terra's health, wisdom, and harm;
Luna's gloss source was well enthroned
    to be
For lovers brought together without effort.


## 11

We went slowly with fervored reasons
    as we entered
The old pillared and stone walled place
Of dancing lights from candles burning
For more purposes than we could know.

We did not go as lovers though that
Would have been our coupled choice;
So we could only imagine those lovers from
    long ago

Also being hesitant as they walked down
That long and imposing ancient aisle.

Surrounded by those old and experienced ones,
And knowing we were carefully encircled
By those who had known our delightful
    hoped for desires;
We no longer wondered whether hopes of any
Live or die in this wise building.

What we learned that day of entering the past
    and our future,
The ones before us also learned fully well.
As long as there are stars beyond counting;
As long as there is infinite sand in the sea;
Love will continue for those who seek this joy.


## 12

This our wedding day is one of desire
With each having nothing more to require
Knowing that all we are to each is clear
And holding to all we want now is dear.

    Come and be with me
    Is my only plea.
    Stay and be mine
    Until the end of time.

We will find in each our fulfilled dreams
Because now we have all needs met it seems.
With happiness the burdens of each we wear
As we realize those things past each will bear.

Come and be with me
Is my only plea.
Stay and be mine
Until the end of time.

May all our days together always be long
While we remember this our wedding song.
There will be a forever with few tears
Hiding in each other leaving out fears.

Come and be with me
Is my only plea.
Stay and be mine
Until the end of time.


13

We find ourselves here as we had once dreamed
Never knowing when we had earlier walked,
Hoping one day we could be together seemed
So far in our future that we just talked.
Today we each know what each has received
From the other which will last for all time,
And our love is far more than we had perceived
As we fully know you and I are mine.
We can now beyond all horizons see
Joyfully together with opened eyes.
We now say with whole hearts come here to me,
And hearing those words know there are no more whys.
    This path we took with no doubts any longer,
    And Canterbury now has made us stronger.

## 14

Those plans we made together wanting
Each to be a part of what would be
    on our wedding day
Now have joyfully come to pass as
In dream-like movements we are finally
    being joined.

I see you standing far away at the end
Of the aisle waiting just for me
To walk toward you my only love.

I see you in your lovely wedding dress
Looking up the aisle toward me
As I stand here with my opened heart.

We feel that time has ceased and that
All moments now have become long hours
    on our wedding day
As we wait so impatiently for all
Our efforts to be completed soon before
    being joined.

I see you smiling as I come closer
To you as I walk up the aisle
With my heart aching for my love.

I see you coming nearer to me
As I wait to put our gold ring
Without end on your finger.

Our voices are strong with love
As we passionately exchange vows
    on our wedding day
Knowing we have found what each

So deeply wanted on our good day of
    being joined.


## 15

We find ourselves once again in this
    lovely paradise
Seeing together the sensual sunrise of
    another day
With the always present turquoise sea
Rimmed by soft sand and all cooled
By gentle trade breezes caressing
This creation through dappled shades
    of palm trees.

Our moonlit walks are under a blanket
    of stars
Along the empty beach with only the
    rhythmic sound
Of the night's sea speaking to lovers
Who exchange kind touches and smiles
With gratefulness of being together
As we are and knowing well the joy
    of this moment.


## 16

### A Wedding Symphony For Lovers

This is finally our day of blessed union,
    and this morning
    I am wondering

If you were unable to sleep as I was unable.
The mere thought of seeing you in a few hours
Thrills me more than I can explain to anyone
Who will listen to me this early morning.

Will I faint from happiness?
Will the priest be there?
Will our rings fit easily?
Will we recite our vows well?

Last evening after dinner your kisses were
warm, sparkling, and golden;
And I could not kiss you often enough as
I saw your ethereal and elegant beauty shining
as my
only star.
You knew that your radiance was reflected
In my face as complete happiness last evening.

I will cherish you.
You are my darling.
We are the other's sun.
I love only you.

The old cathedral sings in the beams of the
Early afternoon sun as it welcomes
the two lovers
for their union.
The tall wooden doors are open asking us
To enter to be made one as others before us.
The stone floor gleams next to the stately rows
Of pews while candles burn far away
Down the aisle of anticipation where the priest
stands in
godly garments.

I see you standing ready
    to walk up to me.
I see you waiting for me
    to walk up to you.
As you approach the altar slowly, I now see
Your smile which overwhelms me with joy.
I can hardly wait to stand next to you up there
Because I now see my handsome one in front of
The ancient altar where we will be joined.
Your hair, your dress, your bouquet of flowers
Shine in the candlelight like welcoming stars.
Finally I am next to you and can see the depth
Of love in your eyes and feel your warm hand.
I confess there in this cathedral that you look
    like a Greek god
    sensuous and strong.

The priest asks me if I take you as my wife,
And there is but one sure answer he will hear.
The priest asks me if I take you as my husband,
And all I want to say is that my arms will always
Hold you as my life will always be warmed by you.

We hear the one in godly garments say the words
We have waited so long to hear;
    those whom God
    has joined together
    let no one
    put asunder.

Did you hear my heart beating? No, I did not
Because I know it was mine beating loudly
    as I realized
    we would now
    always be together
    for the rest

of our lives.
I will always have you in my arms,
And I will always wake up to you;
We will always cherish and love each other
As we begin our dawn together never to part
　　holding our future
　　close to our hearts..

Creator and preserver of all life,
Give them now and for all their time
　　wisdom in their life
So that each may be to the other
　　a strength in need,
　　a counselor in perplexity,
　　a comfort in sorrow,
　　a companion in joy.

Let this always be so for these two now united.


## 17

After falling in love with you, I must leave
　　for some time;
　　I am leaving
　　my fragile heart
　　in your care;
So be tender and take gentle care of it.

You will be taking my heart with you as you leave
　　me here alone;
　　I do promise
　　I will keep
　　yours in my hands
As you will be keeping mine close to you.

Until I return to you, I will hold your heart
    and heal it
    of loneliness
    and give it
    good memories
As I will be thinking of you every lonely day.

We will unite our hearts with eternal love
    when we are
    again together
    after this parting
    for all time
Since we know well we belong only to each.


18

I see and marvel at the wonder of you
    who came into
    my sparse life;
I believed then and more than ever now
    in the goodness
    of your presence
Filling all that I am with your gentleness.

I feel and accept the kindness you offered
    me so freely
    that first day;
I wanted from then on to hold on to our
    good dreams of
    each other
Knowing that our songs are now sung to each.

19

To be loved and be in love we know well
With all its attendants so fully welcomed
In our acceptance of one of the greatest and
    joyful triumphs
    of humanity
As we are united by love with the most
    overwhelming feelings
    created for mankind.


Love is more than the elixir of life;
It is life itself as first designed
For us who accept both joys and challenges
    of something
    so mysterious
That ages of descriptions are unable to find
Words for our summer sun which warms
    us thoroughly
    in winter.


20

Under those cerulean skies where we talked
    of a time
    soon to be
When we would with all joy give to each
Pleasure beyond telling and happiness forever;
We saw our visions of a joined future together;
    becoming now
    so real
As we at last knew the ecstasy of finding
In each what the other always needed.

We find ourselves in another day untouched
    and now new
    for each
Knowing that we no longer have to walk
Alone as we had for too long;
Now our hands are intertwined tightly
    bringing forth
    our renewal
And unmasking well our former visions
While keeping all our hopes so vividly alive.


21


Our love story extends far beyond first moments
And hopes that dreams would become realities
    in our life as
    we placed carefully
    in the accepting
    hands of the other
Our yearning devotion for a fullness neither
Had known before that daring day of discovery.

It cannot be that we do not see each always
Through loving eyes kept open for the other;
Or that we do not embrace the other
With caring hearts ready to accept all.
It is rather that we prohibit with grace
    any diminishing
    of what we
    were given.

## 22

Long before the seas cease their wild
    rush to the shores
    coaxing yearning thoughts,
And long before the moon no more
    hangs gently above
    mother earth and her lovers,
And long before the last raindrop
    falls slowly on
    lonely withering roses;

Let us touch each with that love
The centuries have given man,
And learn of the joys
It has to give you and me
And remember that with this
Those of ages long past
Walked through darkness
In their autumn days.

And let us know that the silver strings
    are stirred again
    to sound their lovely melodies
Through the towers of empty hearts.

## 23

Standing silently amid the mysteries of life
    as the approaching
    time of my leaving
    rushes toward us,
I know my life will be diminished until
We are again together as we had been.

You have assured me that you deeply know
    I will return
    to you who
    keeps my heart,
And that there can be no altering ever
Of your consuming desire for our togetherness.

I have told you so often as I leave you
    I can belong
    to no other
    but my waiting love
Because we are wondrously intertwined to each
For the remainder of our leaving and returning lives.

## 24

Complete love does not lie in escape
    but in true discovery;
Not in finding our paths outward
    but in opening
    our doors inward;
Not in hearing false notes of enticing music
    but in listening
    to our silences;
Not in riding alone over open plains
    but in soaring
    to our secret place;
Not in hoarding moments of personal life
    but in calling
    to each our love;
Not in saving one's own virtue
    but in understanding
    the other's weakness;
Not in building towers in the sun

but in singing songs
through the night of
our complete love.


25


Love is a wild flower
Blown along the road
By a wild wind.

Too often dreams are dreamed only and
        never realized
        for us who
        must dream.
Dreams of love persuade so easily as
We sleep free of what awakening brings.
Love is nowhere; love is everywhere;
And understanding that it is not a destination
But a way is the greatest difficulty for us.
Love can open a heart's closed door
Even if it is an unasked for love
If only the giver and receiver understand
        love is a choice.
Being gentle with another's heart is far
Too often not attempted by either.

Love should support all things in all times
        repairing wrongs
        with easy desire
        to give without hoping
        for anything in return
As it is blown along the road by a wild wind.

## 26

A sorrowful upward way it is that
   pains the heart
   to teach the soul freedom;
Love is always a hard and long way
Even though it is a strong and shining
   liberator of our beings.

Love calls us from our self-made prisons
   only to see not freedom
   but dread wounds;
As love gives us without any hesitation
Our sight only to break our hearts on the
   spectacle of our inhumanity.

Love heals our broken wings when we ask;
   then only watches us
   flying widening circles
Around those endless rows of so many
Other prisons holding other selves caged
   beyond our longing reach.

Love brings to each prisoner's startled hope
   a way to freedom
   and kindness for another
As if invoking any reason for not sharing
What most know should be love's only
   reason to be.

## 27

Somewhere, and it seems always somewhere, beyond
   a first freedom

There must be a necessary dying to defeat and one's
    indulgent pity.
It will never be easy to find living joy within
    those forced boundaries.
Beyond that death is another dawn riding on
Swift winds with promises of a new beginning.
From these strong currents unstable wings
    must leap toward
A phoenix crowned in fire and fashioned with
Signs unreadable for all who dare fly.
One clear high call on the air and this
    reborn one
Soars upward gathering speed unfettered.
It then softly floats down on huge wings
Sweeping over closed doors releasing freedom
    as it swings
      wide the boundaries
      of our darkness.


28


On through the night a bright cloud gathers
    from hill to hill
    from town to town
Flying straight for the bending edge of earth
As it soars into the grey probing reach of dawn.
A great rhythm of pulsating air stirs heaven
    and the highest clouds;
Yet sighs a wind song through deep forests
    on its way.
And from the gloom below grows an answering call
Of mountains and seas; and from above the suns
And galaxies echo now some ancient lost hymn.

Voices of forgotten ages and multiple generations
    call out
For a fierce and remaining love beyond all naming.
This love filling all immeasurable voids and
Hidden worlds above and beneath the stars
Is what quakes the sod and what all seek.


## 29

One blinding stroke of imperious thunder
    throws far back
    every ocean tide
And defies the night pushing wave on wave
Of paling fury down beneath the rising day.
This next one comes riding a newborn sun
    like a white
    blazing stallion.
And we who were once imprisoned here
Soar above an earth crashing upward
To meet a sky now molten.

Then silence and only deafening silence
Fills the cosmic halls and time is done.
The last grain of it falls shimmering
    down the side
    of all space
And dying whispers only of love.


## 30

Upsounding loudly through the curve
    of time

Replacing all knowledge of space in man's
Small stature of existence here in the known
Comes too late for some and too early for others
    that gathering
    that ending
When dreams unrealized die now quickly
Giving way to vistas never seen before.
All collections of love unravel as easily
    as hastily
    woven cloth
Until all that is left is a newness
For those who did understand that
Loving is never the same as living.


## 31


Behind those unavoidable groping corners
Of our restless minds spring inexpressible
    dreams
Made from deep songs stirring from our
Souls needing to be free from bars of no love.
We know that our way can never lie in
    building towers
In the sun of our dreams but in singing songs
    of hope
Through the nights of our dreams so that
We may soar to the promise of full love
Before dawn's grey unassuming herald forces
Us into vaults of spinning newborn suns
Where our timeless dreams die before being
    born again
    to love.

## 32

"I thank you, Father, Lord of heaven and earth . . . "
    Shopping in a store where you saw a
        small child
        in his mother's arms,
    Did you smile at the child and he smiled back?
    Later as you checked out, did the innocent child
    Recognize you as a friend and smiled again?
    Though no words were spoken, you and the child
        knew one another.

"Because you have hidden those things from
the wise and intelligent and revealed them
to infants."
    Friendship with no words is only possible
        with a child
        who knows
    That our world is good and that there is
    Love to be had without effort if we look.
    This acceptance of a stranger seems to be
    Known only to children and not to the wise
        as good.

## 33

Have you heard again this weeping day
The distant and insistent thunder of wings
    becoming weakened
As they struggle to reach your home of love?
You know those tiring wings must soon
    stop
Or they will be forever broken from their
Journey of dreams you placed on them too soon.

Did you think then that love could be a
    burden
While you listened alone to those distant wings
Desperately wanting to bring to you a love
    freely given?


## 34

Walking together in faith is much more than
    knowing;
While knowing the other is useful and necessary,
It lacks mystery and wonder of the other.
Lovers will understand that faith will always
Be a leap into fog rather than into darkness.

With faith in the other in loving togetherness,
    knowledge
Will never be the strength each will need
When loneliness appears in their lives.
Faith imparts without effort for each
The security of never being truly alone.


## 35

It is really not important who taught us
    those years
    of long ago
When we believed we needed little support
For we had the greatest of pleasures in giving to each
    full admiration
    and comfort;
Yet that wise friend recited to us words we had

Never heard before and had never truly realized
    the strength
    given us
By the words of a traditional Apache wedding prayer.

Now you will feel no cold
For each of you will be warmth to the other.
Now there is no more loneliness
For each of you will be companion to the other.
Now enter into the days of your togetherness
And may your days be good and long upon the earth.

So often we have reminded each of those words
    both tender
    and strong
As we have gone down our together road.


## 36

When times moves as slowly as prayed-for rain
    upon a parched
    and desolate earth,
Do we ever see or attempt to understand
What it means for lovers waiting patiently?
Is it always a response to an uncovered situation
    or
Is it a form of exile which always arrives
In many forms deceiving the recipients?
Before time is gone with its promises,
Let lovers know that what is thought
    to be absent
Will always be residing within them.

## 37

Hearing in this morning's early light the calming sound
    of the winds
    through the leaves
Of ancient trees standing proudly along the path
Where we walked that enchanted evening of hope,
We know again the recurring promise which time
    will give
    to those
Who ask and faithfully believe they will receive
What each so ardently desires as a union
Of hearts begins to form where nothing was.
This far vision of being separate but together
Is only shown to those who understand the meaning
    of the great
    call of love.

## 38

Bringing joy out of sorrow and bringing
Wholeness out of brokenness allows us
    to know
    how life
    must be.
Any inability to abide in wonder and awe
Can never be nourishing for our escaping
Time here on this mother of all life.

What is love if it cannot bear the fruit
All mankind desires without boundaries
    of race
    or creed
    or place?

What can love be for any if it does not
Give life both to the giver and the one who
Receives this longed-for moment of being?

Being willing to be amazed at all things
On a daily basis must require a willingness
    to let go
    of one's needs
    and anger
So that instead of being seen as sophisticated;
We can respond with a sense of vulnerability
And then realize the joys of good comfort
As we move from our centered feelings.

39

Taking what we are with our hopes in order
    to become more
    than one,
And aspiring not to being one who feels apart
But connected to another must be done in the sight
Of all around us and much more cogently
    for the one
    who puts
Trust in us through joy unburdened by
Not giving in to the common press of anxiety.

We must understand soulfully that any fresh
    set of opportunities
    to become one
With another must never be taken without
Understanding that this measure of wholeness
Provides us with what we alone cannot do
    and gives us equally

indescribable joy and peace.
This imparts to those who accept this gift
A more robust chorus to proclaim our love.


## 40

Ringing with sounds loudly through all ages
Comes the hope for each that we cannot be alone
    in a chaotic world
    full of wrong choices
Presented as panaceas for everything which could
Be wrong and inexcusable in our challenging journey.

Large changes will always arrive with unexpected
Challenges and more difficulties than we had wanted
    moving from our
    simple singular life
Into something hopeful but unknown to us
In the midst of the going from one way to another.

A better understanding would encompass the knowledge
That we are yet the same person but now having
    a deep humility
    of good togetherness
Which gives us firmly the ability to see that we
Are now not blind and can see beyond our own self.


## 41

Forgiveness will be a constant process
    for those
    who seek it;

It will never be an emotion to be found
Only by the searching fortunate.

We would not be truly whole if we wait
        around for
        some lightness;
And then smugly knowing that we have just
Forgiven a grave wrong done to us long ago.

Sometimes the trauma of a hurtful offense
        can be
        very devastating;
Yet there will be rarely a short route
To forgiveness no matter the depth of the hurt.

Feeling the dissonance between asking someone
        to forgive
        us of our harm;
And all the while knowing it was we who failed
Is never wanting to forgive the other for failing us.


42


Can we envision or truly know that we
        are godlike,
And being godlike must completely mean
For those who know that they are in a
        state of loving?

Though we as created beings live filled
        with errors
And will have to grasp that part of our creation,
It cannot mean that something of our divinity
        is taken away.

Wanting to be loved will be different from
    giving love
Only because we are in a constant flux
Searching for the other created being who will
    make us whole.

When we understand this and accept that
    any ideal
Must be recognized as a goal and not a requirement,
We will then profoundly understand and know
    a great truth.


43


Do we wait in silence so that we are renewed
In good ways which will carry us more gracefully
Through the day as we wait and watch and share
A steadfast love which gives us the strength
    to live into
    better answers?

We must learn to speak companionly with
Each other so that none may feel as outcasts
As we offer both literally and metaphorically
Our love to all who approach us in need
    seeking forgiveness
    and leaving rejection.

There are really those moments where history
Has no end or beginning and where time
Stands still and energy for all never wanes
If we allow our vulnerability and need
    to be far less
    than what we offer.

## 44

Maneuvering through the often chaos of living,
We do ask ourselves in those trying moments
How will it be at all possible to focus on what
    is important
    and not necessary.

Do we actually believe or even understand what
Forgiveness and second chances can mean
To those who most are in great need
    of hope
    and love?

Must we give to everyone who asks us
For something we have and they do not?
What can we do in the face of so much need
    for sharing
    without question?

We should never consider that what we give
May be misused or possibly ignored.
It is in the boundless grace of unbridled love
    that we grow
    and live fully.

## 45

There is that joyful assurance in the confidence
That realized love is in control and can do
    infinitely more than
    we can ever imagine
When we acknowledge that our responsibility
For the guidance of others to that salvation

Of love must have limits.
What we must do is share the love which
    has been given us
    and not earned by us
So that any may know from our life's experience
That all insecurities are deflected and diverted
By the presence of love striving to assist us
To know that our hopeless assumptions
About the future are not for us to repeat
    in this cacophonous place
    we call our minds
    where we must be
    reconciled to our past
    and opened to our present
    so that we are prepared
    for our unknown future.

46

Inviting encouragement and an inclusive love
Which meet people where and how they are
    will create
    something greater
    than what we are.
Guided by compassion found deep inside ourselves
And upheld by human dignity will teach simply
    and firmly
That needed and desired establishment of the joy
Of service to love which all find comforting.
When the holiness and power of love come
To rest in a self-offering person, a new ethic
No longer is a strange circumstance in any life.

Perhaps this becomes the reason we will no longer
    be separated by
    those petty matters
    which are so insignificant
And be joined by a reasonable and common sense
Of that equality created in the beginning.


47


Do we see both our successes and struggles
As meaningful reflections responding not to our
    desperate,
    forgotten,
    impossible,
    or lost causes
But as celebratory intentions and keen awareness
Ever adding color, texture, breadth, and perspective
To that holy place each of us cultivates daily
    within and without ourselves?

Over time we create a cohesive tapestry of identity
For ourselves as we compose a narrative line
While choosing those good things which give
    life,
    hope,
    vitality,
    and promise
Working tirelessly to build an understanding personally
And communally which takes our most
Desperate of fragments and weaves them into
A purpose for our lives.

# 48

How often do we change our minds about something,
    especially something
    we hold firmly
In our hearts such as a long tradition?
How many of us have been challenged to change
Our minds so that we could see others more clearly
    without any prejudice
    of any kind?
What was it that resonated so deeply that it changed
The way we saw both ourselves and all others?

We must reflect on how we treat those whom
    we meet and
    whom we know;
Especially when something goes beyond what we believe.
When we confront someone, we must always ask
Whether we are loving and truly compassionate.
For it is then that we become a fully gracious human.

# 49

We fear nothing as we stand firmly together
Against all who would attempt to tell us
That we have everything out of perspective
    as we dance
    to our own
    tune of life.
We know better than they who can only see
What they know only too well in their
Scattered lives of more downs than ups.
We will continue our good journey
Of knowing the other's needs and pains,

And then doing for the other what will remove
Those upsetting things of life.
We find no effort or problem with the doing
    of what all
    would hope for
    in their together lives.
We find that this joy in careful doing
Provides us with the strength others lack.


50


From all parts of this earth rang joyous chords
Announcing what we knew from our beginning
And what we recognized as being part of this union
    as though our choice
    was now made
    whole by others
    beyond us.
Ringing down upon us were those sounds now
Fashioned as delicately strong bonds around us
So that we would become one rather than two.
Accepting what we heard and felt gave us
    the gracious freedom
    to be only together.


51


Singing through our boundless hearts for each other
Are the ancient songs of joy-produced love
Which always comfort and lift us
    without effort
When we hear them again and again with no

Perception that they have become old and staid.
They are to us as new as the first time we heard
    these songs
Bursting in us with their revelations that we
Would be their instruments throughout our lives
No matter where we chose to journey
    in our life together.
These songs always reaffirm to our being
That whether we are on the peaks of life
Or in the valleys of any despair,
    their comforting presence
    will be with us.


## 52


As the sun rises again over our thoughts
Which race faster than the yellow star,
We once again imagine how our future
    might diverge
    from our past
With those mistakes caused by our indecisions.
What graceful wisdom are we searching for
While we go on with our present walk
    never knowing
    now an outcome?
We realize with clarity that what we now do
Will be magnified in our hopeful future
With either satisfaction or possible regret
    as we cast ourselves
    on the sea of life.

## 53

We both remember so clearly and often
Speak of that marvelous time when our
    first child
    was born,
And how overcome we were with the miracle
Lying quietly in your loving arms
As though announcing to you and me
That she was with us in order to give
Us more joy than we could ever imagine.
Seeing her for the first time far exceeded
Any emotions for anything we had experienced
    at any time
    before our only
    daughter was born.

## 54

Going with you to places near and far
Provides a grandeur which would not
Exist had I gone without you.
You are able to elevate the simple to a stature
    of importance
Because you can see and feel beyond the obvious
And discover much more than I ever could.
Your exclamations of happiness will never cease
To amaze me as we travel to places
    known and unknown.
I realized long ago that you are far better
Than any travel book or guide in pointing out
The often forgotten small things.

Your eyes and our eyes were opened early
    to the great joys
    of journeying to places
    of true wonderment.
Alkmaar, the home of your Oma, was visited
By you at so early an age that it becomes
Difficult to remember all the details of your trips.
In rapid succession came Waterloo with its
Magnificent history you so clearly revelled in.
Rome, the city of great marvels was on
Your list of places to see and enjoy.
Lands End, Oxford, Bamberg, Erlangen,
And so many other places that one forgets them.

    We cannot, however, forget Nuremberg
    With its fairy tale Christmas Village
    Or its euphemistically named
    Documentation Center where dark
    History became brilliant.

We, of course, do remember other places
Such as Phoenix where you helped your
Sister move into her apartment in 114 degree heat.
The Kenai River and its gorgeous salmon along with
Ninilchik where you lugged halibut from the depths
Are truly gracious memories we both share.
There is northern Ontario where you fished in sleet
    in August
    and never
    once complained.
Beaver Lake with your trophy-mounted
Striper and Choctaw Country with plentiful crappie
Must not be forgotten in your angler's journeys.

There are memories of Socorro and on westward
To the Very Large Array and also southeastward
To Trinity Site with all we experienced there
Before the very long trip through Needles to Santa Cruz
    after six years
    in the village
    of Elfago Baca.
Driving and moving from Santa Cruz and your doctorate
To Merced and your post doc research finally ended
On our trip to Santa Clara at long last.

Our journeys provided not only unforgotten
Memories but also forged a bond not to be broken.
Journeys are much more than going in a hurry
    from Point A to Point B;
They unite the travelers while providing each
    knowledge and love.

# IV
## Longings

## 1

I ask myself
    is he thinking
    of me
As I am thinking
    of him,
And then I say I hope.

## 2

I am jealous of your clothes
    for they can caress you
    and I cannot.
I am jealous of your hair
    for it kisses your neck
    and I cannot.
I am jealous of the books you hold
    for they are held by you
    and I am not.

## 3

Searching blindly as though in a thick
    fog along a morning's river
We look everywhere hoping to find
Anything which would comfort us
    on this baffling path
    down through our
    only secure present
Until we have become exhausted and not

Knowing what we have left undone;
    we retrace our steps
    carefully with strength
    knowing now that what
Has eluded us has been with us
All the time in our frenzied looking.
Our hearts knew long before our minds
    that each
    was with
    the other.


4


When lovers ask the other what
    is in this
For me,
The sure and always answer is
    nothing.
When lovers ask the other what
    can I
Give you,
The finding and keeping answer is
    everything.
Some never grasp these solid wisdoms
As they move from one to yet another
Always believing somehow that they
    must always
    focus on
    less love
Than what can so easily be had
    with the other.

## 5

You have as always taught
    me
    something new.
I had believed that there were no
    more lessons of love
To be learned in my life
    with you.
It is so easy to see the ecstasy
    of our being together
    in your eyes,
And I confess I will never tire of that.
We think we can never extinguish this
    love we have for each
As we whisper again and again
Into our welcoming ears
    that we want
    each forever.

## 6

Your lips are like soft pillows
    inviting me
    not to sleep
But to awaken to the joys they give me
As you offer them so freely without
    any hesitations
    or conditions;
And knowing that I need those
Soft pillows so often in my life,
    you tell me
    they are mine
    always.

### 7

Late London streets and uncertain steps
    cannot be enjoyable
Say some nocturnal critics;
But let those be lead as I was
    by a haunting dark-eyed jewel
    with dancing smiles,
And they will know as I do well
The sadness of no more late London streets

### 8

Loving is the only messenger
    which announces life
While we linger in our silence
Where words can resemble those
    moments
Of dimpled time when it becomes too
    late
To know that we are our only hope
In our narrowed hopelessness of no
    tomorrows.

### 9

Why do we now ask as though we
    did not know
Where our joy for each has gone?
It is better that we need to ask
If we somehow somewhere have
    abandoned this joy

which once filled
    our lives
With moments we thought would never
    end?
Or is it far better to ask each boldly
How do we find again what we
    have lost
    through neglect
As we moved too easily in our lives
    together?


## 10


My opened desire is that
There will always be
    tomorrow
When your love is the
    only
Path from this today
Leading to all knowns
Freed from wanderings.


## 11


Were we lost that day of non-seeing
When the other who was yet constant
Wanted only to explain bare truths?
Did our pale thoughts elicit any
    good
Or did we only imagine that our long
    talks

Would bring fully again what was once
    strong?

Surely our wishes were much more than
Needs of hope and grace from earlier
    times
When we knew there were only more
Tomorrows continuing on without flounders
As we in harmony moved on our earth of
    loving.


12


What have I seen this enchanted evening
    as night shadows
    from the street lamp
    distorted not my heart
    but my eager vision?
How I want this moment always to remain
    in my memory
    of seeing the one
    who loves me
    standing there
As though Michelangelo had created him
Just for me and my desires.


13


I saw you almost as though you were
    just beyond
    my grasp
As we met that first time of full wonderment

When neither knew the other.
I felt then a soft despair of not being
Able to see you again even as I hoped
    with my heart
    to remain with you.
Leaving you with my vivid memories
Of our walks during days and nights
Created a hunger I had never known
    before meeting
    you that day.


## 14

I am giving you my only heart
    to hold
    to keep
Close with you in our forever life.
No one has ever had my heart before;
I ask that you will be gentle
With my heart which I give you
    to hold
    to keep.


## 15

Do not think that I am not vulnerable
    for I am
Even though you see me as strong.
I have those feelings which all have
As they fall in love
Hoping the beloved will find in the other
    what was missing

In his life before meeting the one who
    gives her love.
Yes, I am vulnerable and can only find
The strength to live from you.


16


You never asked me that difficult evening,
    though I knew
    so fully
That you wanted to know if I would return
    to you
    ever again.
We saw in each what we had never seen
In anyone else during those precious
    few first days.
Though you did not ask in words,
And I did not answer in words
    whether I
    would return
    or not;
We knew together that I would come back
To you the woman of all my dreams.


17


Can I even dare to think of spending
    one night
    with you
As one soul united by love with hopes
Far more than one long evening together?

Just one night with my only one would be
    as though
    my dreams
Had finally come true in my life.


## 18

Did I fear you would see me as
    I actually was;
Or did I really not know how to tell
    you what you
    meant to me?
What did I miss that day when I first
Saw you standing there wrapped in more
Than I had ever seen before?

How I want that one moment back
So that I could be without fear and
Speak to you as I had wanted
    that first
    day of ours.


## 19

How has it come to this moment
    of parting
When we had always been together
Through so many problems of life?
I wish with all I am that I could
    rewind time
So that we were together again as before.

## 20

All I had to do was close my eyes,
And you always appeared without fail
    in my dreams
    and in my life
As the one who wanted to feel my breath
    on your skin
    or my touch
    on your body.
This desire is much more than any dream;
It is what I welcome and forever need.


## 21

I want to be with you from morning to night
    every day;
Being apart from you grieves me so deeply
That my only thought during these times
    is to ask
    where are you?
I remember the first time ever we parted;
Even knowing we would return to the other
Was not enough to quench my longing for you.
Through the multitude of voices speaking to me
    every day,
I can hear only your dearest voice.


## 22

We each desire so fully to keep
    alive and growing
Those first words of our boundless love.

We fire it gently with our continuing need
    of the other
So that our embers never die and quit.
We know that this refusal to forget
    our first words
Is what now moves us ever closer
With a longing which never ceases.


## 23

I heard tonight a voice from far away
    asking me
    pleading with me
To wrap my loving arms around my only love.
We have followed our dream for each other
    around this world
    separated now by
    time and distance;
Yet we feel still as though we are somehow
Put together by something larger than we.

My only love, my living arms are wrapped so tightly
Around you that I can barely move.


## 24

I heard those plaintive callings of mourning doves
    this shadowed evening
    as I sat alone
    far from my only love;
And though I knew you belonged to no one but me,
There erupted a feeling of loneliness as never before.

As always at these hard moments of living,
I felt this day was born to give us
More pleasure and happiness than we could hold
    on this shadowed evening
    as I sat alone
    far from my only love.

## 25

Come and live with me
And count the stars
    of thousands of
    unforgettable nights.

Come and live with me
And share our love
    with one another
    through all of life.

Come and live with me
And create memories
    for one another
    of our life together.

Come and live with me.

## 26

She left me last night
Giving me her tender kiss.
Can I forget her?

27

Jealous Apollo
Cascaded his wakeful beams
On Venus and me.

28

I remember all too well your last words
    to me
    as you left
That evening of rude shouts and new sorrows
When you were not able to remain with me.

I am now well aware of my many wrongs
    to you
    as you left
That evening of no more promises or hopes
Which you could accept from my lips.

I understand why you could take no more
    from me
That evening leaving far too many good memories
In this empty house and in my desolate heart.

29

Sitting alone here on this cold winter's afternoon
Remembering our summer walks along the paths
    of fragranced flowers
    and flitting butterflies,

I desire two things above all else this gray day
      of no fragranced flowers
      and no flitting butterflies;
I need to hear you tell me just once again
That we will be together in spite of distance
And that we will have summers beyond counting.


30


Fall down rain for ships far
      out to sea
On other tears and thirsty travelers
      bound somewhere
To a forever tideless beach.

Fall down rain for stranded spirits
      barren
Of a stream to carry them on;
      then
Wash away all their many stains.

Weep down rain without stopping
      for me
And carry me soon to sands
      or
Put me finally out to sea.

Fall down and weep down now
      my rain
Of endless love on me for me
      and
Bear me home to love from pain.

## 31

Why is it that time for me now flies
    so softly,
And I know it has left me only when
I reach for today and find it already gone.
Somewhere in another room of the universe
My flown day flashes its color and
    then continues
    itself elsewhere
Leaving empty chairs ringed about with white
Ghosts both of laughter and crying.

If there ever is a new place made for me,
I will search for the ghosts of my flown days
And spend with each a thousand years so that
    I may finally
    know them
Because I never once knew them here.

## 32

All who love must learn early and fully
    that the word
    goodbye
Will leave a deeply vacant place in all hearts
That can never be filled by other words.
Never be haunted by the things left unsaid
    after that word
    goodbye
Has been said knowing there is no way
Time can be made to rewind for anyone.

## 33

These silent nothings which say everything
    always tell us
    when we listen
That without constant love we have nothing
    to keep us
    wanting the other.
Let us now comfort each by our touching
So that we will have nothing to regret.


## 34

There is little need to tell us almost impatiently
That without love and its abundance of
    forgiveness;
There can be made nothing of a life united
No matter what tranquility we possess.

We know well that out of heavy despair
    came hope;
We know well that out of cold ashes
    came life.
We have visited paradise and will never leave
    this choice.


## 35

Do we find ourselves holding back from the other
Those things which should never be thought of
    as rationed
    by either?

Are we afraid sometimes to move forward
When we think doing that will only
    risk new life
    or new possibilities?
We must never remain locked into old patterns
Which only cause doubts and fears;
We should constantly welcome those moments
Urging us to face what we turn away from.


### 36

I am certain I saw it again last evening
    moving along a star lighted pool;
    so lonely appeared this dimmed figure,
    this wisp of damask by the water's edge
    that I knew it must have been my heart.

Alone with no hand to touch or voice to hear
    moved that small part of me;
    as I, remembering other evenings,
    went on without pause though
    hoping this could have been different.


### 37

Those words we said in such unnecessary haste
    yesterday afternoon
    before we thought
    of their harm
Now ring so loudly in our lonely hearts today
That we want time to be reversed to that moment

When we harmed each with careless and angry
    lasting comments
    neither of us
    truly meant
So that we could say with cautious kindness
    what we should have said.



38


Give us once again
The moment of discovery
Which bound us that day.



39


Hearing your familiar voice this early morning
    from the other side
    of this small planet
Wishing me a lovely day on my birthday
And telling me how much you wanted to be
    with me
    but cannot
Caused my heart to stumble and rejoice
    at the same time.



40


I heard yesterday the deep agony in your voice
    as you told me
    with courage
    and kindness

That you were unable to return to me and our home
As we had planned and long hoped for together
Because of a crisis not of your making.

We discussed thoroughly as we have always
    been able to
    the whys
    the whens
    the hows
So that each of us would know what the other
Thought of this unforeseen and unreasonable situation
Forced now on both of us so far apart.


## 41

What vision is here
Holding us with our sad tears
Urging us today?


## 42

Not once have I ever wondered whether I am
    at home
    or gone
Why I miss everything about you.
It does not seem to matter what I am doing
Or where I am doing what I must;
You gently intrude into my thoughts and actions
    like a cooling breeze
    in the summer
    or a warming breeze
    in the winter
    always.

# 43

Not holding my love
Brings to me only despair
Until I hold her.

# 44

I can never hear your voice so far away
    without wishing
That somehow you might also appear
Not as an apparition but as the whole you.
Your voice conjures for me lovely memories
    of when
    we were last
Together as we kissed goodbye and told
    each how
    we loved the other.

# 45

Far away are you
And my only thoughts of you
Is to be closer.

# 46

When will you be back
To my arms and our good home
As I count the days?

# 47

When we have decorated our lover's eyes
    with tears
And have openly wounded a faithful heart,
It is never easy to retrace time and
Redo what should never have been done.
That paradise and that moment have
    been lost
And cannot be recovered as they once were.
Much more than support of the other
Has been relinquished to the thief of joy.
Giving now must be in the full light
    of a desire
      to care
      for the other.

# 48

I am told I walk a different shore
    unable to remember
    names or faces
In the emptiness of an encompassing solitude
From which my life has been drawn.
In the mirror of this sharp existence
I have seen this face before,
And to hide it from exposure
I must walk a different shore
Until I am able to remember names and faces.

## 49

My only wish now
Is for you to be with me
Where we must belong.

## 50

Our apartness must soon come to a
      fully realized
      end;
Or else we will find ourselves bereft
Even of those dreams which now sustain us.
Let us find a way, the way, any way
So that we may once again be together.

## 51

In the mountains of mankind's discontent
Bold rocks squeeze from the earth
      a drop
      and then another
      of grief
And hand them down with ragged hands
To fill the lower pool of sorrow where
      all wait
      with longings
      for the other.

52

Wanting you here now
Is my only deep desire
Again and again.


53

When the heart has sought and finds nowhere to go
Like the frozen hare in the new-blown snow
That seeks for warmth on the hard, cold ground,
   . . . it sits and waits to be found.

When one would come, it looks with glee
Through tearful eyes at who would set it free
And tense with each instant it can hear the beat,
The thump, thump, thump of the oncoming feet,
As an echo makes the sound repeat,
And the biting cold makes fear retreat;
Then at last there is nothing to do but flee.
In concerted howling of the wind and the hound
Comes the infernal beast of the thundering ground.

When the heart has sought and finds nowhere to go
Like the frozen hare in the new-blown snow
That seeks for warmth on the hard, cold ground,
   . . . it sits and waits to be found.


54

Our paths to love stretch far into a gathering
   night

As our dreams elude firmly our hopes of any
    reality.
Ragged voices surround us chanting a heavy
Dirge of hopelessness while we in vain
Seek friendly stars to guide us home to love.
Like starving lions dark messiahs range
    around us
Promising more than can be had in our
    desolated lives,
And all we hear are unknown drumbeats
Firing our minds with rich longings for love.

## 55

You ought not to stay
    too late
    with me
Or it will surely waste
    away
    my heart.

## 56

Our seasons bear always some wisdom with them
As they are a strangely blind accompaniment to our
    moods and fancies.
Those seasons of our lives will sing with us
Or strike an able dirge of warning for us.
But when seasons flee from us so quickly
    without warning
And when storms of living rage out of hand
And when lightning strikes where lightning never was

And when unnamed things hang heavy in the air,
We must beware because more than a change
   is coming.

57

My eyes now so very strained
   in their cages
Strike against a darkened mirror
To find my way to you, and
Must soon cease this effort
Or I will be blind.

58

Where have we forgotten our shared memories
   of times together
   spent in joy;
How should we remember as though from a faraway
Land of joined hopes and dreams of those matters
Which make us whole though separate?

Who did this thing so long beyond all reaches
   of our memories
   of our wishes;
Who blinded us with mystique and smoke
And lethal temple bells sounding so hollow
That all are now buried in elaborate tapestries?

## 59

Leaving you again
Must be similar to death
Since I am dying.

## 60

In those darkened faces of difficulty and doubt
When all we are able to discern well is
    a lack of compassion,
Do we attempt to remember what joy and strength
Bring with their sharing of what we need?
Daring to believe when all odds are far too long
When our community with the one we love
    is broken
    and torn apart
Will keep our hearts open in the wake of pain.

## 61

When our attention is focused on something
    out there
    not here,
Do we understand that something good is lost?
Perhaps that moment of seeking of wanting is only
A misplaced need found here and not there.
For when this happens, we are unable to see
What has constantly been with us all along
    here in front
    of us.

## 62

Bending our times in that corrosive dance
    in which all
    seem to participate
With varying movements suited to our
Needs never quite fit well together
As we yearn so acutely for a pattern
    to follow which
    would lead us
To a harmonious and unified dance of love.

## 63

To find you again
Is my only desire now
As I search each day.

## 64

When was the last time you were totally
    spellbound
By something you were hearing from the one
    you love?
Are there now many times you no longer note
    the urgency
    the beauty
    the power
Of words from the one you say you love?
Capture again the imaginations of those lost words
And relive the power of them in your daily life
With that chosen one whom you say you love.

## 65

Are the words of lovers always said and received
    as they
    were meant
When thoughts became moments of expressions;
Or do lovers only dream that the other must
Have more than his or her only being?
Are prayers fervently said and answers felt
Only because there exists unspoken doubt?
Asking for happiness because of nearness
Can never be a request often granted to lovers.

## 66

Too far from my love
And her smiling lovely face
Hurts me every day.

## 67

To walk laughing with you
Only once again
Is now my only dream
Here in the hard confines
Of my endless memories
Of what had once been
When we were so much in love.

## 68

Love should make us bold enough to reach
    beyond what
    we see
    or feel,
And should make us wonder at all which holds us
Apart from the small and ordinary and dismissible.
Why engage in apocalyptic language which limits
    all lovers
    to unending
    jaundiced squints
When horizons of endless visions present themselves
Through each to each with love for each?

## 69

Wanting you to be
Here with me and not just there
Pierces my sad heart.

## 70

Holding with renewed effort to what we had been
    just a short
    while ago
Will never be in vain as we strive together
To regain what had been given us so frequently.
Running where so many have gone before us
    is not
    our option
As we realize that without the other's presence
Each will become far less than whole.

## 71

Return now to me
Is all I can consider
In my loneliness.

## 72

Love is never meant to be about failing;
But rather it will always be a focus
    on recovering
    from inevitable
Failures and then returning with new strength
To the realities of comforting and reconciling;
And knowing that falling short is what
    we all do.
Understanding that does not disqualify
Anyone from entrenched love as we each
    are constantly
    being polished.

## 73

We must have the strongest of wills
    for one more breath
    for one more prayer
    for one more day
Saving us from relentless remorse of our creating
And finding a way to be kind and loving
    to the only one
    who matters
In our unsatisfied lives we find ourselves.

## 74

Finding each other
Is all that can matter now
Being so apart.

## 75

In the shattered world of those who learned
That the one whom they had committed all
Is no longer the center of their mutual universe,
Comes the dreadful realization through this
    painful awareness
That there cannot be a bridge across this
    great abyss.
While we have boundless belief in ourselves;
We have in us the ability to doubt all
That once had been secure and filled with
    a future.
There is nothing moral about making a promise;
The moral part all must learn is in keeping it.

## 76

We must in our often frantic times of doubt
Be reminded that our strength lies always
    in quietness
    which gives us
    strong confidence
And never in those useless and often hysterical efforts
When we seem to believe that what we see and do
    is not exaggerated.

If we think we have done all to the limit of our
     good abilities,
It is then that we should begin to reconstruct
     our disordered world.


### 77


Holding you so close
Is my greatest desire now
And for tomorrow.


### 78


Holding time as closely as possible means
That hours will not somehow become years
With lost hopes and plans forever vanished
     without knowing
     what happened.
Time does become meaningless when we forget
That nothing can prevent the erosion of it.
When we have gone beyond wanting to use
Our moments with each other and have with no
     regard to any
     consequence
Rashly believed that there will always be time
To do what the other wants, we will discover
     we have failed
     in living.

Needing you today
Is all that keeps me alive
Here so far from you.

Stumbling with only memories to guide you through
    the desolate valleys
While viewing in the distance the peaks of what
    once had been,
Your heart will cry out for a renewal of lost
Desires so that there may be a chance
For your mind to find wisdom which you
    foolishly squandered
On meaningless moments of ignorant falsehoods.
This precious lesson will be given to you
But once with hard definitions which you
    must master.

## 81

Why do you say you are aching to be free
And what is this desired freedom from?
Can you be set free from your perceived
    chains;
Or do you only long to be made whole from
Your brokenness, hurt, and strangeness
Which you say burden you more than
    you can stand?
In the midst of all your self questions and

Through the darkened mirror of things you
    do not now know,
Isn't it possible that those lovely spaces
    of quiet and peace
Can be yours if you accept love that heals
With its new song of wonderment?


82


Now I deeply wish
We were together again
As we once had been.


83


Before parting company with the one whom
    you so certainly
    said you loved,
Is your disagreement about some truly life-changing
Message you may have misinterpreted in haste?
Have you forgotten that love is transforming
And will take precedence in your chaos?
We may feel as though our broken selves
    are too frail
    and too small
To share with another openly and candidly,
But our feeble love is often more than enough.

## 84

Are we deeply certain that time given us
    in all its meanings
Is the central focus of what we now want
    to remove from
    our entangled lives
As we seemingly discuss without any good
And apparent ending to what we think is ungood?
Do we want to find clarity and give each
Encouragement and finally be willing to listen
And be ready to learn fully from the other
As we ask the lost hard questions we forgot
Or is it now that the moment has arrived
When there is no longer any real explanation
    and we must
    move on
    without the other?

## 85

Remembering you
Offers both joy and loss
Since you are not here.

## 86

Do we really let go of our selfishly thinking
    that everything
Must always revolve around our wants, desires,
    and dreams
Wishing only in our fragmented hearts that we

Instead want to be gracious and kind finding
Only that we sense a denial of ourselves
And finally conclude that it is far too difficult
    to let go
    of living
    for ourselves?
Dying to our own devices and desires and living
Into what we think is a sacrificial love will be
The only way to find both grace and love
In our perceived mundane daily life.


87


Holding you again
Is my deepest full desire
While you are not here.


88


Why can't each see in the other someone
Who is gentle, patient, and loving
Instead of believing that the other is somehow
    without any feelings?
Bearing each other in love and living fully
Into the place where each can truly know
    the face and voice
Of someone who cares is far better than
    being apart.

## 89

When we complain, contest, and lament
What we think is the other's seeming
    absence or
    lack of concern or
    unwillingness
Do we understand that these doings in the midst
Of life's most difficult moment for each
Is very real and now, visceral, and vital?
We must know that all the feelings we possess
'    whether good or bad
    average or sublime
    or even downright awful
Are those possessions where we are
And what we actually are feeling.

## 90

We must attempt always to recognize
The message given by another concerning
    an all consuming
    and good love
Which gives up its own desires for the love
    of the other.
When we neglect that fulfilling moment,
It will surely mean that we are seeking
Only what is best for ourselves which
    will lead us
    into a prison
    of isolation
Instead of freedom which comes from that
Understanding of the nature and character of love.

## 91

Are our frequent prayers composed of those
    very necessary words
Which focus our souls on believing in the midst
    of our disbelief
Asking for needed help in our own blindness?
Do we ever ask ourselves why we need
Each other as we stumble on our particular paths?
With incredible mercy and grace we can see
Through the messiness of our lives the hope
    of sustaining love
Which will lead inexorably to a certainty
We feeble humans could not reach with our
    own efforts.

## 92

Remaining alone
Can never be the answer
For our loneliness.

## 93

Do we often confess to our deepest self
That we wish our days could be for us
    much better
With sturdy posts and an accurate fence line
Which would guide us around and through
Those times of indecision and lostness?

We really must learn the great differences
Among those parts of truthfulness which
    can cause
Our lives to become so borderless.

Believing something will constantly mean
Wanting should not be an option anymore than
Knowing is greater than all our wishes.


94


Sometimes the distance between what should be
    and what
    actually is
    can be unbearable
If we do not long to be shown the road we must walk.
Within this constant reminder of our living reality
Will lie the deepest truth of our life's dream
Which often will be in stark contrast to all
That we believe to be absolute truth.
There will be something for each in this search
    which gives
    hope and wholeness
To our broken lives and which will shine
    in our darkness.


95


Could there be another way of viewing reality
    which totally avoids
    both naiveté and cynicism?
Could we look seriously at the way things are

While having an assurance that our present
Circumstances in which we often find ourselves
    do not have
    the final word?
No matter what shadows and rumors we encounter
In our own valleys as we walk in this life,
It will be love which makes all things new.


## 96

Being with my love
Before you can change your mind
Is all that I want.


## 97

Success is such a venerated part of our culture,
    and we seldom
    consider fully
What do we mean when we talk about success.

Left unchecked, we will do violence to ourselves
    and to others
    in the pursuit
Of success in as many manifestations as
    we can imagine.

Is it really important being noticed or being
Someone who thinks he has made something of himself?
Success will be ephemeral at best and
    at worst
    an idol.

A need for significance runs so deeply within
Us that we often mistreat people in order
    to attain something
    not lasting.


## 98

The dark figure often haunting each of us
Is that dangerous thing which causes us
    to lose our place
    skewing our frame
    of steady reference;
That intruding thing in our lives is pride.

Pride will push us to the center of any story
As we become trapped in our own small part
    being isolated
    from any
    offered love
Until we cannot realize how ineffectual and small
    we have become.


## 99

Needing only you
Consumes all my moments now
While you are away.

## 100

Any desire we may at times have
Which causes us to use and possess
    other people
    for our
    own benefit
Can never be a part of what we need in our lives.
This can only mean that we are in pursuit
Of a control of others for the sake of objectifying them.

Is not the opposite a far better choice?
Love is available to each of us and is meant
    to be shared
Without any regard to any human foible.

## 101

When we feel forgotten by the one we love
And ask where love could possibly be
In the midst of all the pain we know;
And as we struggle with depths of uncertainty,
We can find in ourselves the strength
    which enables us
To understand that this very emotion
Must also be only a momentary step
On our journey of living fully.

## 102

Our fear of being a failure in those matters
    of being alive

Must not be seen or felt as letting down
Our families or friends who care for us.

The truth is that when we empty our lives
    of love,
We empty ourselves of all possibilities which
Could lead us on a journey that would be more
Than we could ever hope for or imagine.


## 103

Hearing the voices of those lost from love
Calling for the gates of life to be opened
So that they could rest in the safety
    of a trusting person
Knowing that they could at last have needed peace,
Reminds us that none of us can remain apart
From this human longing which penetrates
Into all that we were and are and will be.
The safety of love given gladly to each of us
Cannot be conquered by anything life presents.


## 104

Do not leave me here
With only my dreams of you
To sustain me now.

## 105

How do we respond when someone we love
    asks us
    for help?
Do we listen with an open heart and offer hope;
Or do we erect those common walls around
Our hearts in order to avoid an answer
The loved one is seeking from us?
If we do, we will end up creating a prison
Where we will become lonely and isolated.

Much better it would be to offer a new perspective
With mercy so that our loved one will see
    an opened door
    which we created.

## 106

Do those once opened doors of endless opportunities
Seem to be closing more frequently now?
Perhaps it is now time to discover the reasons
    that a closed door
    can open quickly
    to something better.
A wonderfully simple way to locate the door
Which will open is to listen to each other
Without rejecting what we believe is a path
Heading to nowhere but more rejection
When actually we will see clearly
    that what
    is cherished
    is now ours.

## 107

Needing you is more
Than all the riches on earth
I can ever have.

## 108

Are you tragically silent struggling to find
Anything that speaks truth to you
As you search relentlessly for answers which
Might calm you and direct you to a measure
    of peace?
You must understand that there are many instances
In which our knowledge of each other is so
Dissimilar that often both are unable to come
    to any agreement.
Being on this well-trodden path should never mean
That we cannot find the grace of love to see
Deeply into the other and be delivered from despair.
Our prayers and our living must be those
    of hope and trust
    which give us
    abundant love.

## 109

We are too often captured by the range of human emotions
And forget that others have also known our personal
    ecstasies and agonies
As they experienced joy, awe, fear, guilt, anger
    vengeance, and love.
One possible way of not being overwhelmed

Is to live a life as well as possible
With an attitude of gratitude for life itself.
Maintaining a grateful heart allows each of us
To see and live past and beyond the current moment
	of all our
	passing emotions
Which can so well destroy who we are.
The next time we are weighed down by anything,
Let us remember to welcome life itself.


## 110

Being without you
Causes me to dream of just you
Until you return.


## 111

Do you seek fleeting solace on those far away shores
	remembering that we are all
	on a journey toward
	becoming new creations
When we are willing to give up everything
We think we own and are owed?
Those objects which our world tells us constantly
Are important
And will fill those depths we have in our hearts
Can never replace whole relationships grounded
In love and support which alone give each
The precious peace we all long for on our journey
	as we seek
	harmony grounded
	in faithful understanding.

## 112

Your always smiling face was so clearly seen
    in the driving rain
On the train's platform we both knew so well
As you stood there watching me leave again
    without knowing when
    there would be a return
    to the other's wanting embrace.
So often we have spoken about and dreamed of
An end to this seemingly forever circle
    where there would be
    a place we could know
    would be there for us
    for all our tomorrows.

## 113

Needing to find you
Is all that now fills my soul
Until I see you.

## 114

Those far thoughts of you haunt me always
Even as they find me running toward your
    lovely memory
    of vivid embraces
And plans for tomorrows full of each other.
I have no way to escape the constancy of those demons
Who pursue me through all boundaries everywhere
    until I am exhausted

with the efforts
to move without
thoughts of you.


### 115

Wanting one more glimpse
Before you left that cold day
Was my only hope.


### 116

Even in the most isolated place or the most desolate state,
        we must know
        we are always
Joined by choirs visible and invisible making all
Our efforts in our thin places become meaningless
As the boundary between heaven and earth prove
        less ephemeral.
There can be no fleeing from that omniscient Presence
Who makes our occasions, places, and moments
        secure everywhere
        at all times.


### 117

Needing you today
Fills my lonely heart so full
Of hope to see you.

## 118

Dreaming of you now
Cannot erase my desire
To hold you again.

## 119

What are we willing to give up so that we may
    live more fully
Admitting that we are oblivious to what is harmful
    and ignorant in our neglect?
By letting go of our selfishness and our desire for control,
And when we are willing to give up everything
    we think we need;
We will find that the holes we have in our hearts
Have been filled with a precious peace which
    fills us each moment
    in our lives.

## 120

When we accept that something once loved
    is over,
We must understand that the time has come
    to move on.
We are tacitly required to let go of the burdened past
In order that we can begin again free of the past.
Grieving the past can never return us to a new day
Which waits patiently to carry us forward
Knowing that our will to persevere comes from
    a mighty strength
    and not from grief.

## 121

Once again I left
Leaving my heart with my love
Where it is so safe.

## 122

Are we living our lives in ways that
    always encourage others;
Or do we find that obstacles seem like
Mountains where our faith becomes too small?
Let us remind ourselves that failure can be a
    humbling experience;
And that each effort we sincerely make teaches us
When times are hard that failure is also a
    great life instructor.

## 123

Remembering you
As I left you once again
Is what keeps me sane.

## 124

When we are apart in distance or thoughts,
    I desire so greatly
    that we might
    once again be together
So that our fractured union might be whole

As we know it must be for us.
I miss the way your fingers move as you
Read another book stopping only to read to me
A sentence or two which you know I will like.
Seeing you so fluidly put together a complicated
Dinner for just the two of us is a stunning
Study in concentration and full purpose.
Missing you is a statement almost shallow
Since there seems to be no words worthy
    of describing all
    that you have
    become in my life.


## 125


Wanting to see you
And knowing I now cannot
Burdens me fully.


## 126


Do you also remember when we first met
    and how we
    could not be
    together enough?
Can you now forget yesterday's foolish quarrel
    about something
    not at all important
    or even meaningful?
Let us find a way out of our strained silences
And avoidances which can only grieve us.
If we do nothing to heal our foolish breach,

We must return to those first good moments
When we could forget and overlook small
Patterns of no consequence before they grew
    into more than
    we ever would
    have dreamed of.


127


My prayer must be
That we will be together
As we were before.


128


I know you told me often with care
That I should not go with them on the trip
So far away from you and our home
Where love and safety have constantly been.
I did not listen to your good words then,
    and now I
    wish I had.
They were in hindsight not the best of companions
Only because they had little regard for the laws
Of that beautiful but distant land of intrigue
Where what they thought was correct behavior
    was not acceptable;
    and now we find
    far too late
    we are guilty.

We were so sorry
That we were to be apart
For those few long weeks.

When we are apart, it is as though
All of time and space has disappeared
And cannot soon enough reappear
    for you and me
    left so alone
    without the other.
All we can do is endure the waiting
Until we are once again with one another,
And then hope that this hard separation
    will not happen
    to you and me
    for a long time.

Knowing you are there
And not here with me today
Casts a dark shadow.

## 132

I know you would have much preferred
To have been with me today
    as I faced
    those difficulties
Which you would have been able to help me with,
But you were unable to go with me
Because you wanted to watch over our home.
When I call you, I will once again
Attempt to tell you how very much I miss you
    and want us
    to remain together
    all our lives.

## 133

Needing you with me
Is a feeling I cannot
Escape nor want to.

## 134

How can I ever forget the immense feelings
    of hopelessness
That chaotic evening we became separated
In the huge airport full of stranded
And angry passengers with no offered help?
I could not see you and needed to see my love.
I could not hear you and needed to hear my love.
That dark feeling of being apart from you
Is an emotion I never want to repeat.

You told me that day
The airplane left without you
And how sad you were.

V

Odes to Hope

## 1

Lonely strengths murmured that night
    as gods might
On those eternal lyres singing melodies
    heard by lovers
who dream as they wonder
    Hoping for more than
    they can find
And thus longing inebriately for other fires.

## 2

No gods but a longing large and strong
    seemed to call them
On their first evening of beginnings
    when they knew
    what they did not
    stepping from too few memories
    of the years past
And seeing darkly into a birth of Hope.

## 3

Saffroned dying day met their glances
    as their minds touched
The Hope hidden in the glade there
    circled by trees
    keeping those secrets
    others might lose
    and never have
While repeating nothing spoken there.

4

Longing tell them for they seek answers
    from your wisdom
On this both a joyful and sad earth
    turned by love
    stopped by hate
    holding gentle wisdom
    for Aphroditian initiates
And giving this Hope to those who ask.

5

This great Hope forever the same
    and yet strangely
For searching mortals never the same
    holds for each
    a tranquility
    returning those thoughts
    of young yesterdays
And never leaving the sought for love.

6

What have they heard from Hope
    this fresh night
On their surely recurring journey
    which will teach solemnly
    what they can
    doubting never repeat
    in this life
And knowing ever have again.

7

When there is longing for the other
    seemingly beyond
All mortal endurance for both,
    and when each despairs
    of being together,
    small efforts with ease
    bring to each
The loving Hope deeply in each.


8

Why does our hunger seem so great
    when all that
Is ever needed is to touch each other
    with all each
    can give openly
    without needing
    anything in return
As Hope rewards us with secure dreams?


9

Lovers who want more of each other
    will learn early
If they are wise and compassionate
    and that love means
    more than words
    and thoughts
    of each other
If they want Hope to dwell in their souls.

## 10

There can be no uncertainties or doubts
    when two lovers
Are found with their giving hearts
    in trusting joy
    with the good
    knowledge of believing
    that the other also
Knows that Hope has truly joined them.


## 11

As long as we have our memories
    of loving times,
Yesterday will remain always with us
    reminding each of
    what was and even
    what was before
    we knew our love
Which now gives Hope for our future.


## 12

Our unspoken words that first time
    gave us
The courage to embrace with joy
    knowing that
    the other also
    removed all doubts
    and unknowns
And our Hope became more than words.

## 13

We embrace Hope knowing that our
    acceptance of this
Never leaves either of us wondering if
    there are limits
    or any reasons
    for what we
    each are doing
As we accept what we have in each other.


## 14

Where have our questions gone which
    seemed to linger
In our learning and younger years
    as we searched
    for answers
    we thought
    the other had
For Hope beyond all our todays?


## 15

Did we understand more than we ever
    thought to Hope
That moment of our first surprised meeting
    when all we
    were able to do
    was stare at
    who was before us
While we knew that the other was there?

## 16

More than ever we know how deeply
    we do love
As we go on through our life together
    holding each
    when the other
    is weakened
    by life's trials
And giving Hope when there was none.


## 17

Finding our long paths of love always
    gives us Hope
That our journey together will have all
    we will need
    for every moment
    both bright and dim
    keeping us
Full of true enjoyment of the other every day.


## 18

As we step out of our imposed prisons
    of our appearances
Laden with heaviness and separations
    which we have
    carried far too
    long in our lives
    every long day,
We meet our Hope for all tomorrows.

## 19

When any doubt appears on our path
    at any time,
We each know so fully well that the end
    of that intrusion
    will leave us
    more quickly
    than it came
Because our Hope in our love is much greater.

## 20

This courageous and totally new song now placed
    in our hearts
Will give us Hope which will constantly endure
    all trials
    all mishaps
    all wonderings
    all fears
As we are now together today and every day.

## 21

Going down our long and sometime difficult
    path of learning
We know intimately that the other is yet
    on our path
    watching for
    obstacles which
    can detour any
Who do not have full Hope on the path.

## 22

Fears that the disparate fortunes of living
    cause undue hesitations
Will bring those who view their being
    where they are
    as moments of
    much less than
    any misfortune
Since they know Hope will sustain them.


## 23

There can be no forlorn forgetting of the other
    as each finds
That the only true solace in their joined life is
    keeping the other
    strong each day
    with words of
    unrestrained Hope
Freely given without urging from the other.


## 24

When those hard moments of all unkind doubts
    come to lovers,
Rescue arrives with a sweeping vengeance
    removing worries
    before they grow
    into more than
    they ever need be
Through the gracious bringing of Hope to each.

## 25

As we live in good fullness our joined life
    of shared love,
We know well that often hard obstacles
    could so easily
    upset our joy
    we seek daily
    from the other;
But Hope rises always to lead us safely.


## 26

When those memories of our low moments
    come to haunt us
As they always seem to do in everyone's life,
    we know now
    that they pass
    us surely as
    the sun overhead
Because Hope removes all that is unworthy.


## 27

We must never forget what we brought
    for each early
As we began building our good united life
    with mistakes often
    and certainly disagreements
    with eager forgiveness
    so that we could
Experience Hope removing from us all errors.

## 28

We know that our love is strongest when it is
    given freely
In the many wonderous forms it takes
    of thoughts and
    of feelings and
    of pleasure and
    of words
So that our Hope for our love is renewed daily.


## 29

When we give freely without ever expecting
    anything in return,
We will always find a missing pleasure
    as we give
    in the absence
    of all Hope
    for something
Which perhaps was always near us anyway.


## 30

Love is not a destination but a way
    to gain knowledge
As we often question what has been given
    to us daily
    by our Hope
    that anything
    moving us
Will be replaced by our chosen way.

31

Let us never consider that those conditions
    which hamper others
Will find their maddening way into our life
    of peace and
    of joy and
    of gladness and
    of love because
We have within us that good Hope of togetherness.


32

When we have heard and seen those distractions
    aimed at us
As we give our several strengths to each
    every moment
    every hour
    every day
    every year,
We know that Hope will always sustain us strongly.


33

There is really nothing which cannot be imagined
    and completed
When a person recognizes that within the mind
    courage waits
    for the person
    to move toward
    all possibilities
Hand in hand with Hope leading the way.

## 34

Too many say it is much easier for them
        never to Hope
That the mishaps they encounter in their lives
        can be overcome
        with prayer
        with belief
        with action
As they attempt to live only on their own.


## 35

Why have so many otherwise good people
        forgotten how
They have been blessed with all they
        want daily
        for all
        their needs
        to live well
Only because Hope is patient and kind?


## 36

We must always remember in our lives
        of uncertainty
When it becomes too easy in rushed days
        to forget
        what we must
        have deeply
        in our hearts
That in uncertain times Hope will guide us.

## 37

When those inevitable and trying moments
    come to us
Without warning or provocation in our lives
    with discomfort
    with loudness
    with accusations
    with lies
We must truly know that Hope will protect us.

## 38

Though distance and the inexorable movement
    of time
May separate us in our need of the other
    for walks
    for talks
    for joy
    for love,
We find Hope in our trying trial of separation.

## 39

The flowing of our tears will always require
    much more
Than repeated words or another welcomed hug
    to stop
    the flow
    of hurt
    and anger;
Telling each Hope is the only known salve.

## 40

Hope gave us the strength to remain
    strong and faithful
When we were forced apart by matters
    not our choosing
    not our desire
    not our prayer
    not our belief
So that we could comfort our family in need.

## 41

Some seem never to understand well or
    even wish to
That without the constant presence of Hope
    no life
    no future
    no memories
    no love
Can anything of any value be in our existence.

## 42

When lovers are captured by questions
    of faithfulness
Which causes even the very strongest
    to doubt
    to wonder
    to reason
    to leave
Only Hope can restore what once was.

## 43

When words mean far less than intended
    and spoken hastily
To the one who should never have heard them
    in the morning
    in the afternoon
    in the evening
    or any time,
Each must remember that Hope always heals.


## 44

When lovers realize that truth without love
    is painful
And when they finally know with certainty
    that love is honesty
    that love is comfort
    that love is openness
    that love is uplifting,
Then they will know Hope is leading them.


## 45

Hope must never be an assumed moment
    in our lives
As we move often too quickly through our days
    of thoughts
    of deadlines
    of problems
    of solutions
Without any understanding of what we have.

## 46

As we continue with full awareness
        of our love
Which has been our firm cornerstone
        in our life
        in our work
        in our rest
        in our home,
We remember our Hope which has been with us.


## 47

When your soul has been unhappily filled
        with grief
Which seems to reside without leaving you
        as you were
        as you desire
        as you plan
        as you pray,
Hope becomes the only solace you can fully trust.


## 48

As we sing our song of love each day
        in our hearts
While we remember how this joy of ours began
        so easily
        so early
        so often
        so completely,
We know that Hope gave us what we have.

# 49

Joyous thoughts of how all lovers finally
    came together
Stir so frequently in the minds of each
    while talking
    while resting
    while walking
    while working
Only because Hope resides firmly in each.

# 50

There can be no undoing of our given time
    in an attempt
To recreate what should have been done well
    at the first
    without effort
    for each one
    with no doubts
When Hope has been in the hearts of lovers.

# 51

As lovers sail through those turbulent and deep seas
    of doubt and despair
Without being able to see any firm shores
    to rescue them
    to relieve them
    to comfort them
    to guide them,
They must always remember Hope will give them wisdom.

## 52

Hope will always be present in the lives
    of patient lovers
Who look beyond their moments of confusion
    which will come
    without warning
    to all who
    profess love
As they move through their together times.


## 53

Hope born of character building for each
    by its very nature
Is empty of self-pity and other burdens
    and fills well
    the unexpected
    moments of life
    with a will
Reminding us of surprise and delight in our lives.


## 54

The one who dares with Hope by his side
    is the person
Who is able to see beyond his present moment
    of confusion
    of doubt
    of hurt
    of question
And know with assurance that all will be well.

55

When lovers make the mistake of turning
    away from talking
About what happened between them recently
    when they were upset
    when they spoke unkind words
    when they left undone matters
    when they became withdrawn;
They must remember that Hope calms all.

56

Hiding from those who have found life as
    full moments of grief
Can never bring undefiled happiness to any
    who can see
    who can hear
    who can dream
    who can change;
Only Hope and devotion to it can establish that lostness.

57

The road which all must travel often has
    detours of choice
Which can cause either elation or sadness
    if made incorrectly
    or made hastily
    or made angrily
    or made thoughtlessly
When one forgets that Hope is always available.

## 58

When there seems to be few full answers
    to our questions
Which we often pose impatiently to each
    on listening
    on learning
    on encouraging
    on loving,
We must know always that Hope keeps us.

## 59

It is often true that what we hear
    has a lot
To do with what daily we want to hear
    from our friends
    from our enemies
    from our religions
    from our lovers
Without finding Hope within our shallow selves.

## 60

Fleeing from those moments of not knowing
    what is good
Can never bring anyone to the knowledge
    of what was wrong
    of how it could be changed
    of why we acted
    of when to reconsider
Without reaching for the guidance of Hope.

## 61

Those remorseful moments which appear
    slowly but surely
When we abandon our knowledge of Hope
    for other beliefs
    for race
    for sexuality
    for ethnicity
Is the exact time when we must question ourselves.


## 62

When we are tested in any manner
    by life,
We can know most assuredly that our
    trials we face
    trust we lose
    grace we forget
    courage we need
Will appear if we allow Hope to be with us.


## 63

Even though we may be small in the sight
    of those we know,
We can still do our part to adding to life
    by sharing
    by caring
    by knowing
    by loving
If we allow Hope to be with our smallness.

# 64

When we pray that we will be mercifully spared
    from life's trials,
And in our asking believe that we will be
    delivered from evil
    protected from harm
    kept from wrong choices
    lifted from joylessness;
It is then that we must invite Hope into our lives.

# 65

When we refuse to surrender to those moments
    of suffering,
Our souls will be refreshed and strengthened
    to withstand pains
    to endure tests
    to withstand temptations
    to overlook wrongs
Only because Hope now resides and presides in us.

# 66

If one is to feel thoroughly known
    and unconditionally loved
With all foibles, failings, and faculties revealed
    with no remorse
    with no shame
    with no shadow
    with no evasion,
Then Hope must penetrate one's being completely.

## 67

The wide door where one always engages
    a place of transfiguration
Will grow wider and perhaps challenging
    without strength
    without guidance
    without wisdom
    without love
Until Hope prepares the door of complete life.

## 68

If you wander through those waterless regions
    looking aimlessly for rest
And unable to find what you believe you need
    as you walk
    as you run
    as you stumble
    as you fall,
Hope is needed to open your doors wide to full living.

## 69

Fleeing through a saddened and heavy life
    cannot be peaceful
Until Hope enters with triumphal strength
    to overcome
    to defeat
    to remove
    to replace
Those long moments of doubt and indecision.

## 70

When we step out in faith and still find
    ourselves stumbling
On our deep journey through this once life
    of doubt
    of desire
    of fright
    of lack,
Only Hope can restore our faith we had lost.


71

Hope will cause the tears streaming down your face
    as you allow the ache
In your heart which so deeply troubles you
    to be soothed
    to be healed
    to be heard
    to be removed
As you give your full attention to hearing this comfort.


72

If we wonder how we can listen
    more closely to others
Who come into our lives often unannounced
    with their despair
    with their tears
    with their wounds
    with their needs,
Always remind yourself that Hope is the answer.

## 73

When lovers have forgotten their beginnings
    and cannot recall
How very much they once cared for the other
    with holding hands
    with slow embraces
    with deep kisses
    with long walks,
They must allow Hope to enter their lives.

## 74

When Hope is always fully in our lives,
    each day becomes
More complete than we could ever imagine
    in our dreams
    in our work
    in our play
    in our love
Because we have given ourselves to something higher.

## 75

Let those who search endlessly in vain every day
    for soothing paths
Remember that only Hope can give what they need
    for their answers
    for their pleads
    for their journeys
    for their futures
Because nothing else can fill that deepest of chasms.

## 76

Among those who refuse to accept assistance
    for any endeavor
Are some who understand that only Hope
    can give help
    can give wisdom
    can give strength
    can give vision
For the trials which come to all who live.


## 77

Facing hard trials in this long journey
    confronts each
As we search for those sound answers
    giving us Hope
    giving us reason
    giving us direction
    giving us wisdom
While we wait often far too impatiently.


## 78

If we ever believe that our lives are lost
    to other forces,
We must look beyond what confronts us so strongly
    with harsh words
    with evil acts
    with sad exclusions
    with sly rumors
And look to Hope to provide a path forward.

## 79

Hope will constantly be available to all
    who seek truthfully
To know the correct answers to those life-altering
    problems of doubt
    problems of love
    problems of hate
    problems of rage
Which all will eventually encounter in life.

## 80

Running from fear of the vast unknowns
    surrounding us
Provides no answers for our questions
    of the future
    of the past
    of the present
    of any time
Until we invoke Hope to join us in our journeys.

# VI
## Epilogues

# 1

My heart has no room to say
    how you have
    lifted me higher
    than I was
Long before you came into
    my lonely life
    empty of
    all feelings.
My heart struggles to understand
    your love
    you have
    given me
Every day since you won my being
    completely
    with your
    elegance.

# 2

What is there about love which
    must include
Missing you?
Does the absence of a touch or
A smile
    mean love is less
    or more
Than before you left me alone
With only memories to keep me
    until you return?

## 3

Are there words enough between us
        to explain
Or is it that reason cannot accept them
        to explain
How we can have and not have
At the same strong time
        each other?
Does reason keep us without hope
Or is our hope the reason
        we are not in despair?

## 4

As long as we have memories,
        yesterday remains.
As long as we have hope,
        tomorrow waits.
As long as we have love,
        today is full.

## 5

As I leave you now,
        remember
That this long trip of mine
        never exceeds our love;
So perhaps there can be no full
        answer
Until lovers know that nothing
Can ever be greater then
        their love.

6

How can two be caught between
  what could have been
And what is their now?
Yearning for what can never be
And hoping for anything to move
  time
Are reflected in true and careful
Words crafted for each other
  knowing
That the wide chasm of time they see
  cannot be bridged.
Creating a world now made
  of time past
And
  of time now
Can only cause the burden of time
To weight ever more heavily
  as she and he
  search
For something for each to cross time
And knowing it will never be.


7


When ravages of inevitable time have
  finally weakened me
And I can no longer hold you as when
  you first captured me;
And when even remembering the hope
Our life together gave us
  has faded
  from my memory;

I will somehow understand at that end
    that you will
    still be with me
Knowing that you told me long ago
You would carry me
    when
I could not walk
    on my own.


8


How I wish I could walk
    once again
    across the streets
    hoping for a glimpse of your shining hair.

How I joyed in seeing you.
You, the one of the always smile.

Now the days are long
And the nights longer;
I walk out as before
    across the streets
    unknowingly hoping for a glimpse
    of your shining hair,

But you are gone.


9


As our days shorten and darken at our end,
    we each know

the other remains
holding the other
as in our beginning
When our days were long and bright.


## 10

Tell me once more of our youngest times
When as in promised visions we knew
the other would
always
be present
Never leaving the other alone in our world.

Tell me once more of our first embrace
In a city foreign to each where we
found more
hope than
we knew
Could ever exist for two finally together.

Tell me once more of the birth of our children
Who gave us much more than we could
dream of
in our
completeness
As we moved along life's long road.

Tell me once more of us.

## 11

As we have grown old together on life's
    far too short
    path of being,
We never forgot those moments of long ago.
Almost as though it was yesterday
    I remember
Our first trembling embrace that late
Afternoon when we found one another.
Going beyond all hopeful dreams,
We began our voyage holding each tightly
Singing in our hearts songs of love
Which grew longer as we grew older.

## 12

Now in our precious twilight always together,
We ask in vain how did our yesterdays go
    too quickly
    too soon?
Our arms which once held each other
So strongly have become burdened with time
And can no longer enfold the other as before.
Memories made from truly glorious moments
Are what now give us strength and hope
    for a few
    more days.

## 13

The joy we have now in our older days
    remained with us
As we moved with love through our
    joined lives,
And today we are enfolded everywhere
With all that we first found
So many good years ago
    in our youth.

## 14

You remain in my sight as though
    we had just met
With your dancing dark eyes fixed
    on me
Who had never seen such beauty.
There can be no recovery from this,
And today you are an eternal spring
    for me.

## 15

Our good life which we have shared
    so abundantly
Had many challenges which we met
    with our love
Because we knew so deeply and well that
    those hard times
Were so minor compared to our
    lasting love

Which we always believed would keep
    us securely together.


16


Though we are now old and weak,
We still without effort daily
    seek
    find
    know
Our hopes of yesterday when we were young
As we rejoice in our dreams made real.


17


We never found it strange during all
    our wonderous
    years together
To remember and talk about those moments
    of long ago
    of our beginnings.
Even now our memories are so clear
That we cannot cease talking about them;
And we know there can never be a time
When we will not remember our first days.


18


There seems little need for us to remind
Ourselves of what holds us so securely
    for it is

what we are
   for the other.
How can there be questions or even doubts
About what has encompassed us for so long
When all we have to do is see the other
   and we know
   without speaking
   what love is.


19


How is it possible that this hard time
   has come
When I must utter those heavy words
   of goodbye
And know that all my tomorrows can never
   be the same
Without the beautiful girl of all my springs
Or the lovely woman of my endless summers
Being with me so full of life and laughter?


20


Our memories are not disturbed by our older days
   or by any matter
   which approaches us
   seen or even unseen
As we hold each other more strongly than ever before
Fending off all moments of every weakness
   before we are caught
   by that hard web
   spun by shortened days.

## 21

Where have our lovely years together gone,
And why did those go far too quickly
    as we lived
    and learned
Not really knowing that time is a cruel enemy
    to all who
    love well?

## 22

Let us fight against these passing days now
As we once fought for our future long ago
    and we will
    continue to live
    and learn.

## 23

We see each other still as we once were
Without considering that we each now are
    no longer young.
That knowledge cannot diminish our true
Feelings for the other as we now see
    each in fullness
    of a firm love
Built carefully through the years under
    our own
    blanket of stars.

24

We now find our time
More precious than all before
While holding more love.

25

As I leave you now
Remember our lovely times
And not my going.

26

Though you cannot hear me this dark day
      in spite of
      my deepest wish,
I know somehow you realize I am still
      with the one
      of my early dreams.
Seeing you so frail is a moment I did not
      want to come
      in our life;
It is now here moving us as nothing ever
Before in our happy decades of being together.

I am here as I have always been
      with you
      only you.

## 27

We each know here in our ending days
That a departure will soon be thrust
　　on our union
　　of so many years,
And we know also that this coming absence
Cannot be avoided by hope, prayers, or anything.


## 28

Though we know yet we live and love
Until living has finally ceased for one
　　leaving the other
　　so very alone
To struggle with that full truth
That no more memories can be made.


## 29

Too many things left
Undone in our hastened life
As we say farewell.


## 30

I am well aware as I know you are,
　　my life's love,
That I simply cannot make it on my own.
So take my worn hand and hold it tightly,
　　my life's love,
And I will fight against my closing days.

## 31

We knew that our beginning must have
    an ending
Even though we willfully denied such a truth.
Many say we are completely inseparable
As we face the finality of our good life
    together.
We have now no understanding how lonely
The other will be facing life alone.
What we do understand and remember well
Is that we wait in our ending
For the other just as we once did
    in our beginning.


## 32

We prayed fervently that what we heard this
    hard morning
Would never come to be in our life together;
But we heard even though the words sounded
    a finality
To everything we have wanted and loved
As we went through our only given time.

As I now descend slowly into my personal sunset,
    and while I can;
I hope with all the strength I have left
That you, my only love, will see a sunrise
    each day
And tell me that until I can no longer understand.

∽ 230 ∽

## 33

Wise ones have said through the ages
That love between two must lead
    to a narrow gate
    of a timeless departure,
And that this moment of deep sorrow
Can be understood as another beginning
    for those two
    who have loved well.

## 34

Why is it difficult for so many to learn
    as we have
That love will always be based on who
    you are
And can never be based for anyone on how
    we look?

## 35

All must learn deeply that time cannot
    be reset;
Nor is it ever possible to resist time.
Nothing in a life well-lived and well-loved
    can ever
    remain the same;
So let all embrace as new seasons all change.

36

When we must sit at our sunset's dawn
And attempt to remember names, places, and objects
     of our early days,
We must walk with courage toward the end
Remaining as close as we ever were.

In our mirror we shared all our good life
We will have seen our faces before;
And now we must not hide from exposure
Because we are walking a different shore
     in our later days.


37

I am thankful that you finally admitted to me
     as I had earlier
     told you candidly
That you no longer have the strength or energy
To do easily those things which you formerly did.
There is neither shame nor remorse in telling the other
What we each knew so frightfully well
     for so long
     but could not
     find the courage
To realize that we now have new paths to walk.


38

Please do not leave me
Alone here without your smile
As a fallen leaf.

## 39

It is so much more important for us as we
    near our end
    together
To be aware of where we have been and how we have
Always supported one another through the decades
Than entertaining those false words which never
    give anything
    but always
    take everything
Which two in love in old age have worked hard for.

## 40

Our first grandchild now
Has entered our last few years
Giving us great joy.

## 41

While we are resting here for a few minutes
On our slow but still sure walks,
Let us recall those times so very long ago
    but somehow
    very near
When we walked quickly with our children
As they impatiently and gleefully ran ahead of us
Knowing that you and I would always be close
    to their laughter
    and their antics
On those joyous walks so very long ago.

42

Nothing is now done
Without the careful knowledge
Of the two who love.


43

We each are so very thankful that we are
Able to remember our past years with clarity
    as we near
    our journey's
    final stop.
We find that those memories of our years
Spent together now give us a strength we
    did not know
We would now need in our later years.


44

The strength we now have
Comes from our life of knowing
That the other was there.


45

Though we wish and pray with all our might
That our remaining time could slow down
    for us,
And though we know and understand so well
That this is physically impossible for all people;

We yet want more time together before there is
    no time
    left for us.


## 46

It must never end
What we began long ago
With our first moment.


## 47

Knowing you are there
Comforts me each time I think
I cannot go on.


## 48

The rain is falling in this evening's dim light
As your tears fell in last morning's bright light
    when we were
    told we would have
Precious few days left to be together
Because of my very advanced illness.

Please do not weep for me in these
Last few days while we are yet together
    as we have always
    been in our lovely life
As we went with hearts joined by an
Unspeakable love for each.

Let us rather find once again the joy
Of memories made when we were young
   and wanted only
    the very best
For the other as we began our life's journey
Hand in hand until we must be parted.


49


Leaving you cannot
Be the last thing I can do
In this lovely life.


50


Leaves now far too brilliant;
Brashly gay they became;
   fly softly
    slowly down
And seem to float on the face of life
Feeding in a lost unconscious memory.


51


Seeing you again
Is all I can now desire
Before I must leave.

## 52

Who forgot to tell you and me the meaning
    of black
In the cosmic color scheme of life?
Who wanted to cast you and me from each
Writhing out of our lovely paradise?
Why are those passive fabrications now
    made known
To us who wanted only to be together always?

## 53

Finding our way together as we face
    our end
Will never be easy for either of us,
But we know fully and without doubt
That the other will be the source of strength
    we need
When that bleakest of times comes to us.

## 54

As one by one the things we once loved to do
    together
    for so long
Become too difficult and slip slowly out of
    our lives,
We do know despite it all with those lost things;
We still will be we as we cherish our wobbly presence.
The strength of this comes from our knowing
That even a diminished life means we are yet
    together.

## 55

Seeing you in pain
When I am unable to help
Is killing my soul.

## 56

I know you saw me yesterday as I
    forgot
    again
What I had wanted to do for you.
I know also that you understand how
I am leaving you slowly every day.
When my mind is clean from the fog,
I am able to see you and remember you
    as before.

## 57

Hoping for more time
To be with the one I love
Is all I now ask.

## 58

We do understand with loving knowledge
That an end will come to all we have
    in each other.
We approach this finality with the same strength

We had in our earlier years when we freely gave
    to each other
What the other needed without prompting.
Though the end of our life together is unthinkable,
We will still be able to give to the other what
    each will need.


### 59

Stay with me just now
Even though we each fully know
You cannot remain.


### 60

Though we both now understand that an end
    must come
And come far too quickly for either of us,
What we cannot know is the immense burden
Which will be thrust onto the remaining one.
We cannot prepare for that time of ending;
Nor can we accept now what it will do
    to the other.
All that we can do now is hold each other
Every day as though it may be the last day
    together.


### 61

I still remember even now in my much
    diminished state

When we were so very young and looking
Forward to our life spread before us to all horizons.
Though now I know I have almost reached the end
    of my part
With the one who shared everything with me,
I will fight to be with you until I have no more
    to give you.


62


Not seeing you now
Is something I never thought
Could ever happen.


63


I never knew what it could be like,
But now I understand far too well
    what it is
    like to be
Hit with hard knowledge of an ending kind
And to be brought to my old knees
By a raw and visceral truth telling me
    that my only love
    is gone forever.


64


How I deeply wish
I could have just a few more
Hours with my darling.

## 65

There can never be a preparation for this coming
    of the lowest
    depths for man
When he is confronted by the flood of events
Which harvest the one left with no regard
For the suffering showered on the lonely one.
These terrifying consequences of having lived
    are hellish
    and abysmal
And can never be avoided by one of the two
Who pledged togetherness until death separates.


66

The fog of lostness descends so starkingly quickly
    and wraps
    the left one
In shards of immediate and wholly insistent pain
While time goes wobbly as though there can never be
    any more time.
The one who remains forgets about everything
Outside the horrible ache which does not leave
As the world seemingly is unconcerned about
    the gaping hole
    placed in the lonely one.


67

Never sweet sorrow
Is this cold final farewell
To all we once had.

## 68

We are faced with ardent and terse language
    telling you and me
    what we knew
Spoken by those who believe profoundly that
This end news must be told immediately
    without kind preamble
So that everyone concerned may now be involved.
We tell each other when we are finally alone that
A broken spirit is more harmful than a broken body;
We say this not only because it is true
But also because we face this now with courage
    from our love
    of many decades.


## 69

Our plans which we have so happily
Talked about now for months to return
To the place we once knew when we first
    met so long ago
Are at last coming true for us.
We know all too well that we do not have
    time on our side
    ever again,
And this journey to our past will be the
Last one for us together always in love.
The memories which we now hold so tightly
Will become realities from our younger times
When we saw each other for that first
    moment of our love.

## 70

With few days now left
Together as we had been
We must not falter.

## 71

Waiting in this desolately empty room
To be informed that the life of my life
    is no more
Becomes so quickly a suffocating hard moment.
How can it be possible that the vibrant person
I knew so well no longer can be with me?
I comprehend well the ending of most things,
But this finality I am unable to grasp
    today or ever.

## 72

Feeling now empty
Since you have left me alone
Creates unknown pains.

## 73

As we now begin this our final journey
    together as always,
We know we will face obstacles never before
Encountered on our beautiful journeys of the past.
We still see in the other the young and desired

person of long ago
When our life stretched beyond all our horizons
Of plans, dreams, hopes, and all we wanted.
Now our horizons are limited and at hand,
And all we can do is rejoice that we had
    those wonderful
     years together.


## 74

The truly unthinkable has arrived far too quickly
    for us
Who thought it could never happen at any time
    to us.
This brutal ending of our life together should
Have waited beyond our knowing of each;
It has come without preparation of any kind
And without any feeling for what we mean
    to each.


## 75

I will leave you soon
With only memories left
Of me for my love.


## 76

There can be no time
When great pain is not a part
Of the end of hope.

## 77

How can our end be twisted into a grimace
    of deep grief
    and hurting agony
As we see in this suffering something that
Forces our eyes to close to the scene?
We are able to find in the other that strength
    forged in love
    over many years
Which now gives us the calming grace needed
    to understand
    and accept.


## 78

I try to imagine what you are feeling
    this desolate morning,
And I am unable ever to understand fully
What you must be thinking even as I am
    humbled by your love.
We are now on a journey which can have
    no good ending
For us who have survived treacherous times
Together as we painted our picture of a life
    of love and faith.


## 79

Nothing is greater
Than the final loss of you
Who loved me so long.

## 80

None of us can claim innocence from knowing
    or living
Free from suffering as we move toward the end.
We all must suffer, and all of us have known
Or will know this final and true pain of life.
We will feel lost in the knowledge that these
    pains and sufferings
Abound in this world where we find ourselves;
And we will learn that the more we lament
The more we can come to see that the life
We are in pain for has had great riches.

## 81

Reaching for my hand and attempting to smile
    as she had
    for our decades
    together,
She told me the lab report identified pancreatic cancer
And that we would now have little time left together.

Her words slammed into me as nothing ever before
    as I tried
    to grasp
    this awful finality,
All the while hoping that there had been a mistake;
And longing to do anything to save her from this destiny.

I cannot understand what is happening here
And I certainly cannot walk this road without her.

## 82

One thing we have asked in our life together,
And one thing we have sought as we lived in joy;
That our final days of being in union
    would be
    filled with
    simple grace
So that our journey would end as it began:
Moments overflowing with unspeakable happiness
As we wait for our welcome to another journey.

Seeing you just now
And hearing your voice again
Is my fervent hope.

Losing you today
Has extinguished all my life
With nothing now left.

Facing this endness from which we cannot escape,
And knowing there can be no tomorrows with plans
    and hopes
Of being together enjoying another day of comfort;
We are richly grateful for all the times of our past

When we laughed and loved and cried as we found
Overflowing happiness in only being with one another.
Now we will soon no longer see or hear the other
    as we had joyfully
    for so many
    blessed years.


86


This thin place where we now find ourselves
    in our quiet
    last moments
Must surely be the gate of Heaven for us.
Perhaps this transitional time merely makes us
More aware that the choices we made together
During our wonderful years now prepare a
Foundation for all that we must now experience.
Our rains will fall and our winds will blow,
But nothing can harm us because our love
    was securely founded
    so very long ago.


87


Sometimes our personal gifts were extraordinary,
And sometimes they were quiet and modest.
As we approach a final parting, we do so
    knowing well
That we have spent our lifetime together
Discovering, developing, and dedicating our gifts
    to each other
    for our common good.

We are now able with humility and grace
Proclaim powerfully without words or deeds
That we part with the comfort of our gifts
    we have given
    always to the other.


88


Holding now those thoughts
Of all our good yesterdays
Makes our end easy.


89


Knowing now what we
Understood so long ago
Gives us now great strength.


90


Shining fully in our hearts now amid
    this desolation
    of no stopping,
We can only find consolation in those yesterdays
When our life together seemed without an ending
And so full of hopeful explorations together
    that we could only
    think of our nows
    and not our thens.
Here in our thens we are thankful for all our nows

Which so richly sustain us in our sorrows
    as we must face
    our unknowns together.


## 91

This moment is not
What either of us had thought
Would ever happen.


## 92

This desperate end
No one can ever avoid
Or even deny.


## 93

Though we know that what we were
Must end for a new thing to start;
And though we know that in order to embrace
    a new something
    a new something better;
We have to let the ending be what it is
So that we can step into the new with joy and awe.

## 94

Leaving my dear love
Can be compared to saying
This world has ended.

## 95

We have found now at our final parting
The sustaining strength of our pervading love
Which long ago captured us so completely
    that without it
    no possibility existed
For our continual and full support of the other.
We know at this lonely moment of no more
That what we had at our beginning
Remains strong at our ending.

## 96

Hold me as I leave
As you did when we first met
That wonderful day.

## 97

No need for those words
Which some think are now needed
Because we lived them.

## 98

Finding at this end time words of encouragement
    and strength
Is not difficult for either of us in our pain
Because we have had a beautiful lifetime
Of practice in thinking, saying, and doing
Those things which help the other; so now
Even when we know one will leave, it is
Never difficult to be as we always were.

## 99

Just once more let me
See you smiling as we talk
About our small things.

## 100

We had so many
Happy times in our long life
And now you are gone.

## 101

This is not what we
Ever could have dreamed happen
To our happy life.

## 102

I am so afraid to tell you what I guess
    you must already
    know with terror
That I have only a few weeks left before
I must leave you forever.
This sorrow overwhelms me with constant
Thoughts of leaving you so very alone.
How can we be so separated after being
    together for so long?
There can never be any preparation for this
Endness which must visit all; yet we had
Always believed that we might escape
    the coming of a
    permanent night
Hoping in vain for forever sunrises.

## 103

Torrents of our tears
Simply cannot remove fear
Of our unknown.

## 104

Please do not tell me you wish you had done
So many other things for me during our life
Together when all we had was very little.
What you gave me then was worth more
Than all the riches of this beautiful world
    because you gave
    without thinking

of yourself.
You gave me more than I could ever have gotten
Had I never met you long ago.
So leave in peace knowing that your
    greatest gift
    to me
    was you.


## 105

I can only hope
That I will leave you in peace
And not filled with doubt.


## 106

I saw your last precious smile you gave me
    this evening
    of great sorrow
In that sterile room where you did not want
    to spend your
    remaining days.
What I would give if only I could reverse
Time to our earlier days of endless laughter
When each day was one of joy not despair.


## 107

These last hard moments
Can never remove our thoughts
From what went before.

## 108

As you held me for one last time
Wanting both my pain to leave
And my life to remain,
I heard so clearly your whisper
That there was nothing you ever
Regretted during our many years together.
Hearing that from my only love
    was the reason
    I briefly hugged
    you tightly
    as before.

## 109

Our very last time
Together is not what we
Had ever imagined.

## 110

Do you remember when we were young
    and very much
    in love
And thought nothing could ever change
What we had in those long ago days?
Now that your end will too soon arrive,
We both still know firmly without doubts
That we remain to this moment
    very much
    in love.

## 111

Entering my room
Where I cannot ever leave
You gave me such hope.

## 112

I saw you there barely breathing
With your beautiful face wracked with pain
In a sterile bed not yours and not mine.
The ghostly memories of other rooms and other beds
    in our shortened union
    cannot provide relief
    from the awful finality
    of all being so wrong.

## 113

When one of us must sit alone,
    as all must,
In a room with darkened memories;
What is the solace for the sorrowed one
    left alone?
Can reading those letters of long ago
    written in joyful times
Or remembering all of our together moments
Remove the relentless pain of a forever
    separation
Which steadily conquers the soul
    so completely?

Printed in the USA
CPSIA information can be obtained
at www.ICGtesting.com
LVHW012057291123
765058LV00015B/1096